PORTFOLIO PENGUIN

MONEY SAVVY KIDS

LORELLA ZANETTI

GORDON PAPE is Canada's leading personal finance expert. The author of several national bestsellers, including *Retirement's Harsh New Realities, Tax-Free Savings Accounts, The Ultimate TFSA Guide, Sleep-Easy Investing*, and *The Retirement Time Bomb*, Pape has spoken at hundreds of seminars in Canada and the United States. He is the publisher of three investment newsletters, *The Income Investor, The Canada Report*, and the *Internet Wealth Builder*. Pape is frequently quoted in the media and is a popular guest on radio and television. Visit Gordon Pape at www.BuildingWealth.ca.

JORDAN KERBEL

DEBORAH KERBEL is the author of several highly-acclaimed young adult novels, including *Lure* (which was shortlisted for the 2011–2012 Manitoba Young Readers' Choice Award), *Girl on the Other Side* (which was shortlisted by the Canadian Library Association for the 2010 YA Book of the Year Award), *Mackenzie, Lost and Found*, and her latest book, *Under the Moon*, a finalist for the 2012 Governor General's Literary Award. She co-authored the bestselling *Quizmas* books with her father, Gordon Pape. Visit Deborah Kerbel at www.deborahkerbel.com.

MONEY
SAVVY
KIDS

The best ways to teach your children
about money for a strong financial future

GORDON PAPE
DEBORAH KERBEL

PORTFOLIO
PENGUIN

PORTFOLIO PENGUIN
an imprint of Penguin Canada

Published by the Penguin Group
Penguin Group (Canada)90 Eglinton Avenue East, Suite 700, Toronto, Ontario, Canada M4P 2Y3

Penguin Group (USA) Inc., 375 Hudson Street, New York, New York 10014, U.S.A.
Penguin Books Ltd, 80 Strand, London WC2R 0RL, England
Penguin Ireland, 25 St Stephen's Green, Dublin 2, Ireland (a division of Penguin Books Ltd)
Penguin Group (Australia), 707 Collins Street, Melbourne, Victoria 3008, Australia
(a division of Pearson Australia Group Pty Ltd)
Penguin Books India Pvt Ltd, 11 Community Centre, Panchsheel Park, New Delhi – 110 017, India
Penguin Group (NZ), 67 Apollo Drive, Rosedale, Auckland 0632, New Zealand
(a division of Pearson New Zealand Ltd)
Penguin Books (South Africa) (Pty) Ltd, 24 Sturdee Avenue, Rosebank,
Johannesburg 2196, South Africa

Penguin Books Ltd, Registered Offices: 80 Strand, London WC2R 0RL, England

First published 2013

1 2 3 4 5 6 7 8 9 10 (WEB)

Copyright © Gordon Pape Enterprises, 2013

Manufactured in Canada.

LIBRARY AND ARCHIVES CANADA CATALOGUING IN PUBLICATION

Pape, Gordon, 1936–
Money savvy kids : the best ways to teach your children about money for a strong financial future /
Gordon Pape and Deborah Kerbel.

Includes bibliographical references and index.

ISBN 978-0-14-318601-4

1. Finance, Personal. 2. Wealth. 3. Money. I. Kerbel, Deborah II. Title.

HG179.P366 2013   332.024   C2012-905173-X

Visit the Penguin Canada website at **www.penguin.ca**

Special and corporate bulk purchase rates available; please see
www.penguin.ca/corporatesales or call 1-800-810-3104, ext. 2477.

To every parent who dreams
of a happy and successful life
for their children

and

To Jonah and Dahlia,
who got their allowance in the end

CONTENTS

· · · · · · · · · · · ·

PREFACE

In October 2011, the British Columbia Securities Commission published the first-ever national survey of student financial literacy. The study, which was carried out by the Innovative Research Group, questioned more than 3,000 recent Canadian high school graduates, most of whom had gone on to post-secondary studies, about their financial knowledge, attitudes, and behaviour.

Some of the results were predictable but others were astonishing. As would be expected, students who had taken courses in financial education were more knowledgeable about issues ranging from budgeting to identity theft. What came as a surprise, however, was their rose-coloured outlook of the world and their unrealistic expectations about the future.

For example, the average student surveyed expected to be earning more than $90,000 in ten years. That's almost three times the actual average for those in the twenty-five to twenty-nine age range with a post-secondary degree. When asked about home ownership, 73 percent said they expected to have their own place within a decade. This is in sharp contrast to the Statistics Canada estimate that about

42 percent of people in the twenty-five to twenty-nine group own a home.

The survey found that just over half of the students were carrying debt averaging about $8,000. Of these, 49 percent said they would definitely or likely pay it off within five years, a degree of optimism the survey authors felt to be unrealistic. "The real numbers tell us a different story," they wrote in the Executive Summary. "Student debt has nearly reached a record high at $15 billion according to the 2010–11 actuarial report released by the Federal Government."

When it came to attitudes, the survey results were generally positive. An overwhelming majority (93 percent) said it was important to learn about money and finances at an early age. The same percentage said that saving should be a high priority.

But when it came to action, the findings were much different. Only 44 percent had a budget while 38 percent admitted they did not know how much money they had earned and spent in the past month. When it came to banking services, 65 percent admitted they had never shopped around and 58 percent were unable to say how much interest they were earning on their accounts. Only 12 percent had a written financial plan.

In short, these kids were talking the talk but not walking the walk.

We hope this book will help change that, at least as far as your own children are concerned. Our focus is not simply on how to teach children about money but, more importantly, how to help them to *live* money—to make its intelligent use a natural part of their daily lives. That means instilling good saving and spending habits, understanding how to find the best value, learning and practising budgeting, and, as they grow older, developing debt-management skills that will steer them away from the financial reefs.

It is also essential that your children develop realistic expectations about their financial future. As we see in the survey results, many young people have no real concept of what their earning power will be or what they can afford to buy. This will eventually lead to disillusionment, frustration, and anger.

The children who will survive and thrive in tomorrow's uncertain world will be those who have knowledge, a realistic outlook, discipline, and adaptability. By the time you finish this book, we hope you will feel equipped to provide them with those qualities—and have fun doing it.

Gordon Pape
Deborah Kerbel
Summer 2012

1
YOUR JOB AS A PARENT

*Today's reality is that much of a child's financial
literacy education occurs in the home. A child's first
experiences with their own money require parental
input, support and guidance if good money
management behaviours are to be established.*
—TRICIA BARRY, FOUNDER AND EXECUTIVE DIRECTOR
OF MONEY SCHOOL CANADA

Being a parent is not easy. In fact, being a *good* parent
may be the hardest thing you are ever challenged to do
in your lifetime.

We all want to be good parents. We want our children
to grow up to be decent people, well-educated, with sound
moral values and a realistic understanding of the world in
which they live.

But helping them to attain those lofty goals is often
frustrating, irritating, and sometimes even counter-
productive. Kids, after all, are people too, and they have
their own ideas of who they are and what they want to be.
Moreover, this self-awareness comes at an increasingly
early age thanks to the stimulus of television, computers,
iPads, and, of course, books.

The problems of raising children are compounded by the bewildering range of knowledge and values that we are supposed to help them absorb and understand. These include family relationships, social skills, religion and morality, nutrition, sexuality, manners, self-awareness, and so much more.

And now we're supposed to teach them about money too? Where does it end?

The answer is—it doesn't. Good parents continue teaching their children for as long as they live, for the simple reason that, even after the children reach adulthood, they continue to make mistakes, just as we did. And as adults, they are often more receptive to the advice and guidance of a loving parent than they were as rebellious teenagers.

So yes, good parents will teach their children about money, just as they will tell them about the birds and the bees when the time is right. And in today's world, understanding the practical basics of money has become a life essential, not a fringe benefit.

As the Financial Planning Standards Council put it in a submission to the federal government's Task Force on Financial Literacy, "Young people must develop a positive relationship with money and learn that their relationship with money is a life skill and as important as their relationship with language, reading, or arithmetic. They need to learn that money is actually a tool to help them achieve what they want in life."

In its final report, published in early 2011, the Task Force stressed the need to introduce courses on basic financial knowledge into the school systems across Canada at an early stage. "Researchers and practitioners told us that financial instruction should start in the early grades to instil good habits and responsible attitudes from a young age, should be reinforced and expanded upon as students progress through their schooling years, and should be supported by parental involvement at home," the Task Force concluded.

Note the last phrase: *should be supported by parental involvement at home*. Even if school systems do adopt the Task Force's recommendations (and that may be a long time coming) it doesn't let you off the hook. But as matters stand right now, there is no early-childhood financial education in most schools—in fact, there is none at all on a mandatory basis in many systems right through to high-school graduation. Unless parents step in, we'll raise yet another generation of financial illiterates.

We say another generation because until now every cohort of young people entering the workforce has been, as a group, financially incompetent. There are exceptions, of course, but most young people finishing high school don't have any idea about how to prepare a budget, shop for a loan, invest money, or deal with credit card debt. Why? Because no one ever taught them the fundamentals.

This is nothing new. Both of the authors of this book grew up with little if any parental guidance when it came to money management.

GORDON'S STORY

If my parents ever tried to teach me about money, I cannot remember it. Looking back, it appears the subject was taboo in our house. My mother and father never discussed family finances in front of me (I'm not sure they even talked about it with each other) and never attempted to help me understand the value of money or how to handle it.

Everything I learned was self-taught through experience. At the time, we lived in rural Michigan just a few steps away from a popular Lake Michigan beach. During the summer when the cottagers would come up from Chicago, old Pat Walsh would open his little store just down the road. I first learned the value of money there. A piece of bubble gum cost a penny. A Coke or an ice cream cone was a nickel. A loaf of bread, which my mother would send me to buy every second day, was a dime. It was because of that little store that I learned what things cost and the values of coins at a very early age.

I also found that when I asked my parents to buy me something at Pat's Place, as the store was called, the money wasn't always forthcoming. I had to find some way of earning it myself. One day when I was in the store with my nose pressed against the glass case as I stared at a Milky Way candy bar I couldn't pay for, Pat came out from the back. The little store also acted as the Western Union telegraph office for the neighbourhood, and a wire had just come in for the Hamilton family who lived up on the hill. Pat couldn't leave the shop—would I take it to them? Pat was always kind to me and, not having anything else to do besides staring at the unattainable Milky Way, I agreed. When I got to the house, imagine my surprise when Mrs. Hamilton asked me to wait a minute and came back with a quarter tip. I was thrilled, raced back to the store, and bought my Milky Way. I was perhaps eight at the time, and this was the first money I had ever earned. From then on, I became Pat's telegram delivery boy. Not everyone tipped quarters—that was a lot of money back in the 1940s—but I always got at least a nickel.

My parents didn't object, but neither did they offer any advice on what to do with my tips nor did they suggest saving any money. The closest they came was to give me a piggy bank one Christmas. I figured out the savings part for myself after that.

The telegram incident taught me about the gratification that having a little money can bring. Having experienced it, I wanted more. I became a mini-entrepreneur. My first venture was setting up a lemonade stand at our front gate but that flopped—Pat's Place down the road also had lemonade and a lot more. Then I tried using my little stand to sell my old comic books. That went a little better, but I found I couldn't get more than two cents per comic from the stingy cottage kids. I couldn't buy much with that. It was only when I accidentally hit on the idea of selling worms to visiting fishermen that the money began to roll in. More on that in another chapter.

My teenage years were spent in Trois-Rivières, Quebec. Nothing much changed at home; my parents still didn't talk to me about money. But I understood that we had very little of it when we moved into a one-bedroom rented apartment over a store on a downtown commercial street and I had to sleep on the living room sofa. Then my mother was stricken by a paralyzing stroke, and the cost of providing her with home care wiped out any savings my father may have had.

With virtually no money available for me, I began working summer jobs at an early age. At first, it was only to earn spending money to carry me through the year. As I got older, I realized I wanted to go on to college. My father strongly opposed the idea—I think now it was because he couldn't afford it, but he never said as much. So I began to save some of my summer earnings. After finishing high school, I worked for a full year and saved most of my salary, which, combined with a small scholarship, was enough to get me through my first year at Ottawa's Carleton College (now University).

It was then that I learned how to budget. Again, no one taught me, I had to work it out for myself. It was either that or starve. So I figured out how much money I could afford to spend each month on food, rent, transportation, and so on. In subsequent years, I got a part-time job at Carleton as assistant to the athletic director, which, combined with my summer work, enabled me to earn enough to get my degree.

At that point, I was in my early twenties. I had learned the value of money, how to earn it, and how to budget all by myself. I never had a single lesson on the subject in school and had no guidance from my parents. Looking back, I realize I was fortunate to have enough of a practical mind and a head for numbers to enable me to get through. But I also understand how little I really knew of the financial complexities of the world when the education system finally finished with me. It was many years before I really gained a thorough understanding of money management. Unfortunately, like my own parents, I never succeeded in imparting that knowledge to my own children.

DEBORAH'S STORY

Before I begin, I think it's only fair to explain that my dad wasn't always a financial expert. It wasn't until I was fifteen or sixteen that he started writing articles and books about money. The truth is that, for most of my childhood, neither he nor my mother knew much about finances. So, when it came to teaching me and my two siblings about money, Mom and Dad were just trying to figure it all out as they went along. Kind of like most of us.

I remember my first allowance was twenty-five cents a week. I was about six years old at the time and it was just enough to buy myself a package of Starburst Fruit Chews at the local store. Raises in allowance came annually on my birthday and were usually in amounts of twenty-five cents. I was receiving a dollar a week by my ninth birthday— which seemed like a lot of money at the time. Once it was spent, that was it. There was no asking my parents for more. It was either wait until the next "payday" or resort to desperate measures. On hot summer afternoons, I can distinctly remember scouring the sidewalks and curbs with my best friend Joanne, both of us hoping to find enough dropped change to buy ourselves a ten-cent Popsicle at Beckers. Sometimes we were successful. Sometimes not.

During these years, I had a Mickey Mouse bank that I loved. The bank had four clear plastic tubes for arms and legs and a torso with a rudimentary sorting mechanism inside. When you inserted a coin in Mickey's head, it was sorted by weight and dropped down into the appropriate arm or leg slot depending on whether is was a penny, nickel, dime, or quarter (remember, there were only four kinds of coins in circulation back then—the loonie and toonie were still years away, and people didn't use half-dollars—and still don't). The back of the bank was made of see-through plastic so I could watch each coin travel through the sorting process. Back in the days before iPads and Wiis (heck, this was even back before Sony Walkmans and Atari) when the only children's programming on TV was on Saturday morning, this bank was a great source of entertainment. Today's kids would barely bat an eyelash, but it was one of my favourite toys. Every week I'd collect my allowance and put it in my Mickey Mouse bank. Sometimes I'd spend it, and sometimes I wouldn't. But there was certainly no suggestion from either of my parents that I try to save any of it.

When Cabbage Patch Kids became all the rage, I decided I wanted one—badly. From what I can remember, the doll cost thirty-six dollars—a veritable fortune in my eleven-year-old world. My parents made a deal with me: if

I could come up with half the money, they'd pay the other half.

Looking back, it was a noble plan, although tragically flawed in execution (sorry, Dad). At eleven years old, I had no means beside my meagre allowance to earn the extra cash I needed in order to be able to afford my doll. So, after gleaning a couple of dollars in change from every overturned couch pillow in our house, I did the only thing I could think of to procure the rest of the money. I begged. Not on the streets of course, but in the comfort of my own home. Whenever my parents had friends over, I'd bring out my homemade, crudely fashioned "collection box" and solicit donations for my cause. Over the few weeks or so it took me to reach my goal amount, I'm sure my parents were wishing they had come up with a different plan. But they weren't the kind of parents to go back on their word, and within a few weeks I had collected enough for my half of the purchase.

Perhaps it was the begging fiasco of the Cabbage Patch Doll that motivated it, but a year later my parents announced they were starting a new initiative in our home. They were scrapping the old allowance system that had been in place and instead would start paying us a set rate for each job we would do around the house. Two dollars for vacuuming the living room. Three dollars for sweeping the floors. Three dollars for dusting the furniture. In this way, my siblings and I would have the option to earn as much money as we wanted. My dad provided us with a "sign-up sheet" so we could decide between us who would do what.

Of course, my older sister and brother snatched up all the choice jobs before I ever had a chance to get a word in edgewise. Such is the fate of the youngest child.

As a result, I was left cleaning the toilets to earn my spending money in those days. Luckily for me, I was less than a year away from getting my babysitting certificate and, soon enough, that became my major source of income. Bye-bye, toilets!

My first real job outside the house was at Sam the Record Man in the Bayview Village mall in what was then the North York borough of Toronto. I was hired as extra staff for the Christmas season, working for minimum wage. I don't even think I had a title. I was just ordered to assist the legions of clueless adults who were looking to buy cassettes or CDs (which were just getting popular) for the teenagers in their lives. After that, various retail jobs followed over the years and, by the time I was ready to head off to university, I'd saved enough to pay for my first year.

Now, here I am married with two kids, eking out a living as a novelist for teens, and facing the daunting prospect of teaching my own little ones about money. When my dad asked me to co-author this book with him, I agreed mostly because it would be a great opportunity to school myself on the subject. My oldest child had just started asking for an allowance, and I had no idea how to answer him.

When we began researching this book, my children were ages five and eight, and neither had ever received an allowance before. They did have money saved from birthdays, Tooth Fairy visits, and grandparent indulgences. But they didn't do a lot of spending so the money just sat in their piggy banks. Whenever there was something they wanted, they would ask us to buy it for them. Often we'd say no, but sometimes we'd say yes. And sometimes we'd tell them to put it on their birthday list, and they would receive it as a gift. In the end, our kids seemed satisfied with this system, and we didn't feel the need to offer an allowance.

When my son first asked for an allowance, my first reaction was "no." Why did he need more money than he already had? It's not as if he spends what's in his piggy bank, anyway. And it's not as if he's really wanting for anything. I cringed at the idea of him wasting money, hassling me to take him to the store, and ultimately bringing more "junk" into our home. We said no and the subject was summarily dropped.

The subject came up again a few months later when my son found out I was writing this book. "Please can I have an allowance? All my friends get one." This time we weren't so quick to say no. I told him honestly that I really didn't know if an allowance was a good idea or not, but I would research it, talk it over with his father, and by the time the book was finished we'd have an answer for him. Jonah decided this was okay with him and has been patiently waiting for me to let him know what I've come up with.

THE SEVEN MONEY COMMANDMENTS

If you are going to have any success in helping your children understand money, there are some basic rules you must follow. We call these The Seven Money Commandments, and it is important that you adhere to them at all times, no matter how great the temptation may be to give in "just this once." Here they are.

Thou shall not spoil the child

In some ways, it is worse for children to have well-off parents than to be part of a family that is always scraping to make ends meet. Affluent parents are more likely to be overly generous with their children, granting their every wish. The end result is a child who comes to believe that every desire will be fulfilled simply by asking for it. These kids will be in for a terrible shock when they discover the real world doesn't work that way. It's your job to make sure your kids understand that going to a store doesn't always mean buying something. Don't give into every whim. Remember, saying no doesn't make you a bad parent. Quite the opposite: it means you're setting limits and sticking to them and, in the process, teaching your child some valuable life lessons.

Thou shall never give in to whining

Every child does it. Some become masters at it. Whining: one of the banes of parenthood. Whining children can become so irritating that parents will give in to their demands just to get some relief. DON'T DO IT! Every concession will only reinforce a child's conviction that whining gets results. This is especially true when it comes to money. The parent who buys the candy bar in the grocery store to stop a child's whining is only setting herself up for more of the same. As for the child, she will come to believe there's no need to do any work to get something she wants or even to behave well. Some well-timed and very loud whines will do the job just fine.

Thou shall not succumb to guilt trips

"But Dad, Joey has one." "Come on, Mom, all the kids are going." "Don't you guys want me to look nice in school?" Every parent has experienced it—the guilt trip children try to lay on you to get you to cave in to their demands. Sometimes their arguments are so cleverly crafted that you begin to seriously question your own motives and start second-guessing your decisions. That's exactly what the kids want. As long as you have carefully thought out the decision before answering, stick to your guns. You have nothing to feel guilty about.

Thou shall not be an automatic nay-sayer

If your immediate reaction is to say no every time a child asks for something, you're setting yourself up for trouble. Every request is not unreasonable, so some should be granted. It's a matter of deciding which have merit and it may take a little time, and perhaps some spousal consultation, to decide. By automatically saying no, you put yourself in the position of having to reverse your position if you later decide to grant the request. Your child will quickly come to understand that no doesn't always mean no, and you'll be in for a world of hurt as a result. Your best reply is something along the lines of "we'll see" or "I'll talk to your mom about it." Then follow up—most times, the child won't forget and will come back in an hour or two wanting an answer.

Thou shall not contradict thy spouse
Never allow a child to play one parent off against the other when asking for something. That's a sure way to stoke family tensions and to encourage manipulative behaviour in a youngster. Even if you don't agree with your spouse's decision, you must be supportive and help devise a rationale for why it is valid. If parents find they often disagree on these matters, they should resolve to discuss them in private before making a final decision.

Thou shall not be unreasonable
Children will often be unreasonable in demanding things, whether it be a toy, an ice cream cone, or a new dress. That doesn't mean you, the parent, should be unreasonable too. As with just about everything else associated with child-rearing, there's a fine balance that has to be struck. Never forget that your child is a person. She wants things, just as you do. But, like you, she can't have everything she wants. You have to decide what is reasonable, both for her needs and your pocketbook.

Thou shall practise what thou preach

You and your partner are the primary role models for your children so you need to lead by example. The "do-as-I-say-not-as-I-do" ploy isn't good enough. If you want your children to be good money managers, you have to show them the way. More on this later in the chapter.

YOU CAN'T TEACH WHAT YOU DON'T KNOW

"Dad, can you help me with these algorithms?"

"What's an algorithm?"

Obviously, you can't teach your children what you don't know yourself, whether it's math, geography, astronomy, or money.

This means that a large number of parents are ill-equipped to help their children learn the basics of money management. According to the International Adult Literacy and Skills Survey conducted in 2003, almost half of all Canadians "struggle with simple tasks involving math and numbers." A more recent poll conducted in 2011 by the Ontario-based Investor Education Fund found that only 29 percent of respondents scored well on a test that asked twenty-three basic questions about investing and personal finance.

These results shouldn't come as a surprise. With most education systems still hesitant to add courses in personal finance to the curriculum, it's hardly a shock that the majority of adult Canadians are, to put it politely, under-informed when it comes to money management.

How about you? Do you have enough basic knowledge to give your kids at least a working understanding of money? Try this little test on the next page and see. Couples should take it together. Answer each question with yes, no, or don't know/not applicable and check the scoring system that follows.

SCORING: Count one point for every *yes* answer to odd-numbered questions (1, 3, 5, etc.) Count two points for every *yes* answer to even-number questions (2, 4, 6, etc.) Subtract one point for each *no* answer. Score zero points for any *don't know* responses. A perfect score is 24. Now check your results on this scale.

SCORE 18–24. Excellent. You are well-equipped to help your children obtain a solid grounding in financial matters, and you have probably already started the process.

SCORE 12–17. Good. You have reasonable knowledge and enough practical experience to get the kids on the right path. However, it wouldn't hurt to learn more about those aspects of finance in which you're weak.

SCORE 7–11. Fair. You have some knowledge of personal finance but you probably are short on applying it. You need to improve your own understanding before trying to teach your children anything beyond the basics.

SCORE 0–6. Poor. Don't get down on yourself if you are in this group. Based on the surveys, you have a lot of company. The important thing is to recognize the shortcomings and do something about them.

HOW MUCH DO YOU KNOW ABOUT MONEY?

	Yes	No	Don't Know/ N.A.	Score
1. We have a family budget				
2. We stick to our budget				
3. We know how much debt we have				
4. We know how much debt interest we pay				
5. We file our tax returns on time				
6. We complete our own tax returns				
7. We save some money every month				
8. We have invested some money				
9. We know what an RESP is				
10. We have opened an RESP				
11. We know what RRSPs and TFSAs are				
12. We have one or more RRSPs				
13. We want our children to be financially literate				
14. We encourage our children to earn their own money				
15. We are teaching our children about money				
16. We have opened bank accounts for our children				
Total score				

GORDON'S FINANCIAL FUNDAMENTALS

Some years ago, when our first grandchild was about two, my wife, Shirley, bundled her into a car seat and drove off to pick up her mom from a doctor's appointment. Unfortunately, Shirley missed the turn-off to the medical building, at which point she uttered an expletive in her frustration, which I will politely modify here as "Oh s**t."

Immediately from the back seat she heard a tiny voice repeatedly saying "Oh s**t, oh s**t, oh s**t, oh s**t." Our granddaughter was just learning the delights of speech and was mimicking everything she heard. She didn't let up when her mom got into the car: "Oh s**t, oh s**t, oh s**t, oh s**t." Needless to say, Shirley was devastated and found herself apologizing repeatedly to our daughter for her verbal indiscretion.

Children are greatly influenced for good or bad by the words and actions of their parents and grandparents. In business, executives are told to lead by example. The same is true in the home. If you don't want children to use bad language, don't use it yourself. If you don't want them to smoke, kick the habit, if you have it. If you want them to learn how to handle money properly, make sure you are doing it yourself.

The reality is that many adult Canadians are poor money managers. They don't budget properly, they run up credit card debt, they fail to save for the future. If you want to help your kids avoid your mistakes when they grow up, you have to start by dealing with your own bad habits.

Your first priorities should be budgeting and saving. Not only are these essential for good family money management, but they are the easiest concepts to pass on to children at an early age. Here are some tips.

Budgeting

Okay, budgets are boring. Let's get that out of the way up front. That's why some people will use any possible excuse to avoid the perceived drudgery of creating and monitoring a family budget. But if you don't budget yourself, how do you expect to convince the kids to do so?

The concept of budgeting is hardly rocket science. Very simply, it's a method of allocating family income in an efficient way and monitoring the results to ensure that everything stays on track. The most effective approach is to prepare a budget for each month and then update it once a week so you can identify problems before they get out of hand.

The easiest way to do this is by using a budget spreadsheet. You don't have to design it yourself as there are several available on-line. We offer a free Excel budget spreadsheet on our Buildingwealth.com website at www.buildingwealth.ca/PersonalFinance/FamilyBudget.cfm. There's also a very good one at a terrific Canadian website called Golden Girl Finance; the link is www.goldengirl finance.ca/budget.

You can find other examples at www.kiplinger.com/tools/budget, www.vertex42.com/ExcelTemplates/family-budget-planner.html, and www.budgetworksheets.org.

If you have Excel 2003 or a later version on your computer, you can download one hundred budget templates at http://office.microsoft.com/en-us/templates/CL102207099.aspx?CTT=97. These include family budgets, personal budgets, college budgets, travel budgets, wedding budgets, home renovation budgets—you name it and they probably have a template for it.

The notable exception is a children's budget. But since kids and computers have a natural affinity, it should be easy to create a simple one they can use. You'll find an example later in this book.

The starting point is to show your child how your own budget works on your computer. Don't go into too much detail. Simply explain how you set aside a certain amount of money each month for housing, food, clothing, transportation, savings, etc. Then suggest they try the same thing with their own money—allowance, gifts, earnings, and so on. You'll find a free simple template you can use at www.millionaire-kids.com/support-files/childrensbudgetworksheet.pdf. It's in a pdf format, but you can easily adapt it to any spreadsheet. Once the kids see you managing the family money this way, the chances are they will want to try it themselves. And when they do, they will have taken the first step towards a lifetime of good money management.

Savings

Grandma always told us that we should put something aside for a rainy day. Unfortunately, many people are ignoring the advice of that wise old lady. According to the Vanier Institute of the Family, in 1990 the average Canadian family saved about $8,000, which worked out to a savings rate of 13 percent. By 2010, the amount of money saved each year per household had plunged to $2,500, for a saving rate of 4.2 percent. No wonder personal debt levels have been steadily rising!

Most parents encourage their kids to start saving from an early age, the piggy bank being the iconic symbol of childhood frugality. But how much conviction can you bring to the savings message if you're not practising it yourself? Remember, kids learn by example and you're their number one teacher.

Author David Chilton (*The Wealthy Barber*) and other financial experts advise putting aside 10 percent of your income before you make any other financial allocations. ("Pay yourself first.") If you think you can't afford that much, start with what is comfortable and add to it. Obviously, most of that money will go into the bank but why not also have a mommy/daddy piggy bank when the children are very young? Make a deal with them: for every dime they put into their banks, you'll add a quarter, or a dollar, to yours. It can become a weekly ritual—they put money into their piggy banks and then come and help you deposit some coins into yours.

When the time comes, the piggy banks can be emptied and the children can come with you to the bank and open their own accounts.

Gordon's experiences

Virtually every parent has experienced the stress of trying to cope with pleading, tantrums, sulks, and anger from unhappy children who want more money to buy something that they believe is absolutely essential for their continued existence. It may be anything from a candy bar to a video game, but at that given moment it is the most important thing in the world, and woe betide the parent who withholds the cash needed to acquire it.

As a parent of three and grandfather of nine, I've had ample opportunity to try various techniques for dealing with this problem. None have been completely successful, but some have worked better than others. One thing I have learned is that you cannot apply the same formula to each child. Each will respond differently, depending on his or her age and temperament. So you'll need to be flexible, to the extent that's possible while trying to remain even-handed and treating each child fairly.

One thing I did discover is that timing is everything when it comes to your kids and money. Avoid trying to do too much too soon. That's a mistake I made with my own family. My lack of early financial training undoubtedly contributed to it; I didn't want my children to grow up with bad money habits because of a failure on my part to give them the grounding they needed. So I started pushing things sooner than I should have and ended up turning them off.

Preteens simply aren't ready for complex financial information. Most of them can't handle anything more complicated than allowances, a bank account, a basic budget, and some simple explanations of the relationship between value and money.

. . . .

Quantity, not quality

Young children do not intuitively grasp the idea of quantity versus quality. To them, more is better, whatever it is. That was brought home to me when we sent some money for the fourth birthday of one of my grandsons, with instructions that it should be used to take him shopping for something he really wanted.

The father told the boy about it and showed him the cheque.

"Where do you want to spend it?" dad asked.

"The dollar store," came the instant reply. "I can buy more things there."

His parents used the opportunity to develop the idea of value in his mind. They pointed out that while he could get many small toys at the dollar store, he could also use his birthday money to buy a starter computer. The child had been fascinated by computers and the games that could be played on them for several months and immediately understood the trade-off that was being suggested. He eventually chose the computer and has had good use out of it ever since.

. . . .

Very young children see something they want, and they expect you to get it for them. Trying to painstakingly explain to a two-year-old that Mom and Dad can't afford that expensive doll right now is not likely to have much impact. All the child will take away from your explanation is "no," and she'll react in her usual way to the negative, depending on how badly she wants the doll.

You have to be the judge of when your children are ready to learn the basic principles of money. It might be as young as three years or it may not be until the youngsters are five or six, depending on their intelligence, perception, and maturity. When you begin, introduce the concept gently. Make it a game that the child will enjoy playing. You'll find lots of ideas in the Money Babies chapter.

It's around the time children hit their teens that they become more sensitive to the subtleties of money management. This often coincides with a first job or a highly prized but expensive objective they want to achieve, such as owning their own iPad or laptop. That's the point at which you can start going beyond the basics in laying the groundwork for a more sophisticated approach to money and wealth.

You're going to have to commit some of your time and imagination to the process, though. You can't just hand them a copy of a book and tell them to read it. It will sit unopened on the shelf, as I learned from experience. The time will come when they'll seek out more information on their own and absorb it avidly. But not at the outset.

OPEN AN RESP

Your children may still be very young, but it is never too soon to start saving for their post-secondary education. That's one of your parental responsibilities, and it needs to be taken seriously.

University costs are already sky-high and will certainly continue to move higher—cash-strapped governments simply don't have the money to significantly increase payments to post-secondary institutions. For a real eye-opener on university costs, try out the University Cost and Debt Calculator on the Investor Education Fund website at www.getsmarteraboutmoney.ca. Pick any university you want across Canada, choose a degree, and get ready for a shock when you see how much it will cost. For example, a four-year engineering degree from the University of British Columbia will cost $64,160 based on 2008–09 Statistics Canada figures on student expenses. A four-year education diploma from Acadia University in Nova Scotia will set you back a mind-blowing $76,656! And those prices will be much higher when your youngsters are ready for college.

Those numbers are providing an incentive for more parents to make it a priority to start putting money aside for their children's future while the children are still very young. It's a smart move because, unless the child is scholarship material, she may not be able to afford post-secondary education or may end up heavily in debt as a result of student loans. I get email all the time from graduates who are struggling to pay off the debt load they built up while in university. It's especially difficult if you're starting a family at the same time.

One of the best ways to put aside money for education purposes is a registered education savings plan (RESP). They have some drawbacks, but they've been greatly improved in recent years, and the addition of the Canada Education Savings Grant (CESG) means the federal government contributes to your child's university fund.

RESPs have been around for many years. However, they didn't attract a lot of interest from Canadian parents until the mid 1990s when university tuition fees began to skyrocket and articles started appearing in the newspapers about the heavy student loan debt loads many graduates had incurred by the time they received a degree.

An RESP is a government-approved tax shelter specifically designed for education savings. However, despite the similarity in name, it operates quite differently from its cousins, the registered retirement savings plan (RRSP) and the Tax-Free Savings Account (TFSA). For example, contributions to an RESP are not tax-deductible, unlike an RRSP. Any money that goes into the plan is contributed on an after-tax basis, the same way as TFSA contributions. Once in the RESP, any future investment income that is earned is tax-sheltered. However, when a student withdraws cash to fund his education, the income is taxable in his hands, unlike a TFSA withdrawal, which is tax free.

You may set up an RESP for your child at any time. There is no maximum annual contribution (that rule was changed in 2007), but the total cumulative amount of the contributions cannot exceed $50,000 per child. RESP contributions must be made by December 31 of any year. Note this is a different deadline than that which applies to RRSPs. Contributions may be made for up to thirty-one years after a plan has been opened and the RESP must be wound up by the end of the year that marks the thirty-fifth anniversary of its creation. If the money has not been used for education purposes at that time, special rules come into play. You can create either a family plan, which covers all of your children, or a specified plan for one child. RESPs can be set up by parents, grandparents, other relatives, even public agencies responsible for the upbringing of children.

Although the Income Tax Act says the proceeds from an RESP must be used for education, there are no hard and fast rules as to what costs it actually covers. Generally speaking, education payments include tuition fees, books, equipment, lab fees, student fees, sports fees, accommodation, and transportation. As long as the payment can reasonably be associated with post-secondary education, there should be no problem.

The one major limitation is a ceiling of $5,000 that can be withdrawn as an educational assistance payment (EAP) during the first thirteen weeks a student is enrolled in a qualifying educational program. After that, there is no limit on the amount that can be withdrawn as long as the student continues to attend school.

The Canada Education Savings Grant

The Canada Education Savings Grant (CESG) was introduced in the 1998 federal budget. Under it, Ottawa adds an extra 20 percent to your annual RESP contribution each year, up to a maximum of $500 annually per beneficiary. So you need to put at least $2,500 into the plan each year to qualify for the maximum payment. The maximum lifetime grant per child is $7,200, which equates to $500 a year for 14.4 years. Your child is entitled to the CESG from birth through to age seventeen.

There is a bonus amount for lower-income families. If net family income is $41,544 or less (2011 figures), the CESG may be increased by a maximum of $100 per child to $600 a year. For families with net income in the range of $41,545 to $83,088, the maximum annual CSSG is $550 annually. The $7,200 lifetime maximum still applies. Another support program for low-income families is the Canada Learning Bond, which is worth up to $2,000 for the RESP. Alberta and Quebec offer supplemental programs that can add to the plan.

CESG and Canada Learning Bond payments are made directly to the RESP, not to the parent or the child personally.

. . . .

CESG is popular

As of the end of 2010, 42.8 percent of all Canadian children between the ages of zero and 17 had received some money from the Canada Education Savings Grant.

. . . .

RESP risks

If your child does not go on to post-secondary studies and there is no one else who can be substituted as a beneficiary, you have a problem. The original capital can be withdrawn, because it was paid with after-tax dollars. But the earnings and the CESG are another matter. If the beneficiary does not go to college, the CESG must be paid back to the government. As for the rest of the money, the rules are complex.

If you have RRSP room available, the money can be transferred there. Otherwise, it must be withdrawn in the form of what is known as an accumulated income payment (AIP). You will be assessed tax on the withdrawal at your marginal rate plus a 20 percent penalty unless you live in Quebec, in which case the penalty is 12 percent. That means most of the earned income could end up in the government's hands. Before setting up a plan, make sure you understand exactly what will happen to the accumulated interest if your child doesn't turn out to be university material.

One way to reduce the risk is to set up a family plan if you have more than one child. It will cover all the children in your family, so if one decides not to go on to university, the others can benefit from the extra money (although the CESG for children who do not go on to higher learning will have to be returned). This at least provides a measure of protection against having the government snatch most of it back twenty years or so down the road.

It's important to remember that all contributions that the parents make over the years can be withdrawn tax free. It's a good idea to take out your capital before the student starts collecting EAP to keep the tax picture clean. Remember, any money withdrawn by the student is subject to tax. Don't run the risk of having your principal subject to tax when you can take it out of the plan tax free. If you then want to give the cash to the student as a gift, you can do so with no tax consequences as long as he is no longer a minor.

Where to invest

Setting up an RESP is simply a matter of paperwork and making that first contribution. The tough part is deciding how to invest the money. There are three possible approaches.

Dull but safe. If the number one priority is to protect the plan from loss, this is the route you'll choose. The portfolio will gradually increase in value through a combination of your contributions and the Canada Education Savings Grant, but the invested money will earn very little because low risk equates to low return. Your best choice in this situation is guaranteed investment certificates (GICs), which are covered by deposit insurance. A slightly more risky but potentially more profitable choice is bond funds, either mutual funds or ETFs (exchange-traded funds).

The middle ground. These securities carry more risk but also offer the prospect of better returns. So over time the value of the RESP may increase by a much larger amount. For example if you contribute $2,500 a year to an RESP for ten years and the CESG adds another $500, the plan will be worth $33,506 after a decade if the return averages 2 percent annually. But if you can obtain an average return of 5 percent, the RESP will be worth an additional $6,000 at the end of that time.

Obviously, you don't want to take big chances with your child's education money. The best route is to choose an ETF or mutual fund with a strong record of long-term growth and moderate risk. Balanced funds (which invest in both stocks and bonds) are a good compromise if this is the way you want to go. Some that fit the bill are CI Signature High Income Fund, Fidelity Canadian Balanced Fund, and TD Monthly Income Fund.

Go for growth. If the soaring cost of university has you worried, you may decide to aim for the best possible return from the RESP, consistent with not turning it into your child's equivalent of a Las Vegas casino. An average annual compound rate of return of 8 percent would grow to almost $47,000 after ten years, based on a $3,000 annual contribution and CESG. That's more than $13,000 better than investing in 2 percent GICs.

The trade-off is risk. If stock markets crash, it may take the RESP years to recover. During the meltdown of 2008–09, some high-risk mutual funds lost 40 percent and more. Your child may be too young to understand any of that, but you're not.

The funds that performed best over the past decade tended to focus on small company stocks (small-caps), natural resources, and emerging markets. But what worked best in the past may not perform well in the future. Resource stocks, for example, are notoriously cyclical, recording big gains for a period of time and then plunging in value.

A small-cap fund may be the best choice in this situation. They offer a diverse portfolio of small and medium-size companies, and some also include U.S. stocks in their mix. Dynamic Small Business Fund and Beutel Goodman Small Cap Fund are two excellent examples.

Our recommendation is that you use a combination of all three of these strategies over the life of the RESP. If you open the RESP when your child is very young, use the first ten years to maximize returns. When the child turns ten, begin to move to lower-risk investments such as balanced funds. Once you reach the point where college or university is less than three years away, switch to GICs and/or bond funds to protect the assets in the plan against an unfortunately timed stock market crash. Don't risk losing a large chunk of the money by staying aggressive for too long.

Scholarship trusts

RESPs that are marketed as "scholarship trusts" have caused concern for securities regulators for several years because of the high up-front fees that participants are asked to pay and the penalties that are applied if payments are missed, the plan is cancelled, or the student does not go on to post-secondary studies or drops out after the first year.

The Canadian Securities Administrators (CSA), an organization that brings together representatives of all provincial and territorial securities commissions, has proposed requiring full disclosure of "the costs and risks that are unique to scholarship plan investments." The costs include "front-loaded enrolment fees," which can be hundreds or even thousands of dollars. "The risks relate to failing to maintain the prescribed payments and the beneficiary not attending a qualifying educational program," the CSA says.

If the new rules have not been implemented by the time you go RESP shopping, make sure you insist on receiving a complete break-down, in writing, of all fees and expenses associated with any scholarship trust you might consider.

RESPs set up at banks, credit unions, and brokerage firms normally carry very low fees.

SUMMING UP

Your job teaching your kids about money isn't easy—but then, nothing about parenting is. However, the fact you picked up this book at all says you are serious about helping your children be good money managers and hopefully avoid the financial problems so many people experience as they get older.

Begin by updating your own financial knowledge and improving your money management habits, if necessary, so that you are well prepared to take on the challenges of teaching your kids the basics. They're not going to learn this in school—the responsibility is on your shoulders. In the following chapters, we'll give you advice and tips on how to handle it.

2
MONEY BABIES—AGES 5-6

A penny means one, a dime means ten, and …
what's that one with the beaver on it?

—DAHLIA, AGE SIX

GETTING READY

Yes, your baby's growing up. At this age, your little sweetheart has a year or two of preschool under her tiny belt, is becoming more and more independent every day, has learned to count simple numbers, and is busily figuring out the ins and outs of the world around her.

In other words, now is the perfect time to introduce the concept of money.

Although she still might seem like a baby in many ways, believe it or not this is the right time to begin. Deborah's daughter Dahlia was five years old at the time we started researching this book. It was the perfect age to jump in with the basics. Any sooner and the lessons would have been too difficult for her to grasp—something her big brother had already figured out and had been taking full advantage of. Here's the story.

Deborah writes: I made an unfortunate discovery one morning while walking by Dahlia's bedroom. I found my then four-year-old girl, at her then seven-year-old brother's suggestion, emptying her piggy bank and happily giving all her coins away to him, as freely as if she was tossing confetti.

But once she turned five, all of that was behind her (much to her brother's dismay). That's because, for the first time in her young life, she started to grasp the concept that items have value. In other words, the coins in her piggy bank weren't confetti after all!

Until this stage, most young children are blissfully unaware that certain objects have a higher worth than others—something the jaded adults in their lives sometimes forget. On the morning of his third birthday, I remember asking my son Jonah what he wanted most in the world. Not having any idea that there was a shiny red tricycle awaiting him in the garage, he thought about the question for a minute before answering, so innocently: "a leaf."

To this day, I laugh at this story. Yes, we could have saved ourselves a lot of money on the tricycle and just picked him a beautiful leaf. At that age, he would have been just as happy. But those innocent days are fleeting, and before you know it your wide-eyed toddler has become a world-savvy kid and is asking for iPads, Wii systems, and hockey tickets.

Sadly, leaves don't cut it for long in our consumer-driven society.

As many young parents can attest, the kindergarten years are generally seen as the beginning of the "buy-me, I-want-it" stage. And, as parents of older children can attest, the "I-wants" get bigger and more expensive with every passing year. Understanding the concept of money is the first step in helping your child realize that she wasn't born with an all-access pass to the world's toy stores (or clothing stores, or electronics stores …).

. . . .

Money quote

There is no doubt that early behaviour and skill development are essential in ensuring lifelong financial success.—Stephen Ashworth, President and CEO (Acting) of Junior Achievement, Canada

. . . .

To help them understand the ABCs of money, they'll need some hands-on experience. This is the age when your child should be learning what money looks like, what it feels like, what it's used for, and how to count it.

HOW-TO

So, how do you teach your Money Baby the basics of spending and saving? It's best to start, as Julie Andrews once famously sang, at the very beginning. Be sure to go slowly and help your child learn in ways that are developmentally appropriate.

Play with her

At the ages of five to six, your little Money Baby can count simple numbers and is starting to enjoy sorting things by colour, shape, and size. She might have even lost a tooth or two and been left a gift of "spare change" from the Tooth Fairy. Small, shiny, and tactile, it almost goes without saying that this is a perfect time to introduce her to coins. Children of this age learn through play so be sure to make any kind of "lesson" fun.

Help her get familiar with money before the real lesson begins. Start by getting down on the floor with your child. Empty coins onto the carpet and have her sort them into piles by colour and then by size, going from smallest to largest. When they've been sorted, show her the "pictures" on each coin and explain how each one has a different value. With the tiny dime being the smallest coin, she'll naturally jump to the conclusion that it's worth the least, so she'll likely need a few reminders.

Here's an easy way to help your Money Baby remember the different value of regular circulation coins.

Maple Leaves = penny = 1 cent
Beaver = nickel = 5 cents
Bluenose Schooner = dime = 10 cents
Caribou = quarter = 25 cents
Canadian coat of arms = half dollar = 50 cents
Loon = loonie = 1 dollar = 100 cents
Polar Bear = toonie = 2 dollars = 200 cents

Turn them all "queen-side" up and play a simplified game of Memory. *Where's the caribou hiding? Where's the beaver? How much is the polar bear worth?*

She'll have fun trying to remember. And if she gets stuck, help her out and move on to the next one. You may have to play these games a few times before the lesson is learned.

Once she's got the coins mastered, see if she can sort them into piles according to their worth. When that's done, try stacking them up high, counting as you go, and seeing who can make the most "expensive" or tallest tower. Then knock them all down and start again.

With six-year-olds, you can try raising the level of difficulty by explaining the idea of equivalents. Show her how five pennies equal one nickel, two nickels equal one dime, four quarters equal one dollar, and so on. Be sure to have real coins on hand for this because nothing beats a visual demonstration. At the age of six, you can also move on to explaining the various denominations of bills. (You'll find that these will be much easier for your child to learn, as the value is more visible than on the coins.)

Now try making it real by helping her understand the relative value of things. Place several items on the kitchen table that she'll be familiar with. Make them as varied as possible. For example, an apple, a candy bar, a toothbrush, one of her hats, a favourite toy or game, a pencil, a book, and a pair of socks. Make sure you know the approximate price of each item. Give your daughter some coins and a five-dollar bill and tell her you're going to play store. Ask her what she wants to buy from the "store" you've set up and how much she is willing to pay you for it. Tell her that once she has used all the money you've placed in front of her, the store will close and she won't be able to buy anything more. Also say that you will only sell her the item if she offers a fair price.

Let her choose the first item she wants and make an offer. It will probably be way off the mark, so this is when you explain to her what the item would cost in a real store and ask if she still wants it. If she says yes, take the money and tell her to choose again. As the game progresses, she will quickly catch on to the fact that some things cost much more than others and become more selective in how she spends her money.

. . . .

Tooth treasure

Did you know that the average child loses her first baby tooth around age six? A recent survey by Visa Canada found that 80 percent of Canadian children receive between one and two dollars from the Tooth Fairy. By the time she's a teenager, your child will have lost twenty baby teeth and made a nice, tidy profit along the way. With the coins piling up under her little pillow, all the more reason to start your Money Baby on the right path to understanding money.

. . . .

Take her shopping

Now that she has learned to handle money and done some play shopping, it's time to take the next big step. Seeing money in action is another important stage in helping your child grasp how it works. As we all know, little children love to help their parents (teens, of course, are another story entirely). So when your preschooler accompanies you to the grocery store, why not let her participate in the payment? Children love to feel like they're doing something "grown-up," and this can be a fun way to reinforce the lesson that there's an exchange of commodities going on … that you must pay money for the things you want to purchase.

. . . .

Making change

Deborah writes: The idea of receiving change can be puzzling for young children if it's not explained carefully. A clear understanding of coins and bills is essential for a child to grasp this concept.

For example, I remember a time when, after seeing me pay for an item with a twenty-dollar bill and watching me receive a ten, a five, and a handful of coins back, Dahlia was understandably confused. "You gave the man one piece of money, why is he giving you six pieces back? That's not fair."

Obviously, at that point, I hadn't done a good enough job explaining the different denominations of money.

Hey, we all make mistakes, right?

. . . .

When Dahlia was five, she used to enjoy sitting perched on the store counter, watching the cashier ring in the purchases, and then being allowed to hand over the credit card to pay for it all (don't worry, we stopped short of letting her sign the receipt). As she's grown older, she's graduated to handling coins and bills and watching as the cashier makes change and hands it back.

Remember, this is the age where "fairness" becomes important. Following rules as well as the ideas of "right" and "wrong" are also a big part of how your child sees the world. The concept of a "fair" exchange of goods will make all kinds of sense to your Money Baby if explained properly.

Take that lesson a step further when you're at the super-market or corner store. If you find a price that you feel is too high, take a minute to point it out to your Money Baby. "I don't think that's a fair price for this item. Maybe if they lower the price, we can think about coming back to buy it."

As soon as you feel like she's ready for the next step, it's time for the dollar store. Give your child five dollars—preferably in loonies—and take her to the dollar store (where it's pretty much a given that most prices are fair). On the way, explain how she can choose five items … one for each loonie. Unless your Money Baby asks, don't worry about explaining the concept of tax at this point—that will come a bit later. The purpose of this exercise is to reinforce the value of money, the idea of a budget, and the process of paying for goods.

Once your Money Baby has confidently mastered all the different denominations of coins and you feel her counting skills are up to the task, give her the five dollars in different combinations of coins and take her back to the dollar store for a second round. Give her a little purse with four quarters, ten dimes, one loonie, twenty nickels (don't bother with the pennies unless you want to unnecessarily frustrate both your child and the cashier) and see if she can sort out the payment at the cash register.

The Disney World experiment

Deborah writes: My husband and I took a similar kind of approach when we went with Jonah and Dahlia (age nine and six at the time) on a family vacation to Disney World. We were excited about the trip but we were also a bit leery of the overabundance of toys and treats we knew would tempt our children. In hopes of avoiding a bombardment of "I-wants" and "can-I-haves," we decided to give each of our children a shopping budget—a predetermined amount of money to spend on souvenirs and Disney memorabilia over the course of the trip. We agreed that each child would receive twenty dollars for every day we were in the park and that they could spend it however they wanted (with no judgment or interference from us).

The plan worked beautifully.

Not only did we avoid being nagged by our children, we had them comparing prices, thinking ahead, weighing decisions, and calculating numbers—all while on vacation! It was fascinating to watch their different approaches to the situation. Jonah whooped for joy when he heard how much money he was going to be able to spend while we were away.

(Remember, twenty dollars a day might sound like a lot at first, but it doesn't actually go very far in a place like Disney World). Although he never once asked us "Can I have …?" he popped in and out of various toy stores over the course of the six days we were there. He took his time, scouted out the items he wanted most, all the while carefully calculating how much he could afford to spend on each one. By the time our last morning at Disney arrived, Jonah had managed to spend it all—down to the very last dollar. It was a triumph of precision budgeting pulled off by a child who'd turned nine only a week beforehand.

Dahlia, who had only just graduated from senior kindergarten, took a more cautious approach with her budget. Also, considering her age, she needed some help from us with the math. "How much money would I have left if I bought this?" she'd ask, weighing her various options as we meandered through the toy shops. Worried she might run out of money if she spent too quickly, she was careful to only buy the things she really, *really* wanted. A balloon, a doll, some charms for her bracelet, a little pearl from the Japan pavilion in Epcot. In the end, Dahlia ended up spending less than half the money in her budget. But she was proud of the choices she'd made and happy with the freedom she'd had to make those choices.

By the time our Disney World trip was over, both my kids were thrilled with their purchases. And we were thrilled with the maturity, thoughtfulness, and self-control they'd displayed over the course of the holiday. It made us think that an allowance might just be a good thing after all.

But we'll discuss that further in the next section.

None of this would have worked, by the way, if our kids hadn't been brought up with the firm understanding that "no means no." My husband and I have always been very careful to let them know that "we mean what we say and we'll stand by it until we can't stand anymore."

If you don't do this in your home, I highly recommend you start now. Children who think they can wear you down with crying, pouting, nagging, whining, and asking incessantly—will! We also taught our children the notion that entering a store doesn't necessarily mean we're going to be buying something.

The sad saga of the unicorn

Deborah writes: Here's a funny story that underscores just how hard it can be to stick to your guns. When Dahlia was four years old (and only in school for half days), I had to take her on an errand to a local bookstore to pick up a gift for one of her cousins. Knowing that I would have to walk through the store's toy section in order to reach the children's book section, I prepared Dahlia ahead of time for the errand. "We're only going to the store to buy a book for Rachel, okay? We won't be getting anything for ourselves. Mummy won't be buying anything for you on this shopping trip, so please don't ask me. Do you understand?"

Dahlia assured me that she understood. And, since she'd always been such a mature and reasonable child, I felt confident we could pull it off. So in we went. Everything was fine, until we passed the toy section and Dahlia spotted a fluffy white stuffed unicorn—complete with pink horn, shiny, pastel ribbons, and pleading blue eyes. Dahlia dropped my hand, ran to the unicorn, pulled it off the shelf, and held on tight.

The tears started falling before I even knew what was happening. All my careful preparation was blown out the window.

"Please, Mummy! I NEED him!"

I gently extracted the little unicorn from her grasp and quietly reminded of her of the purpose of our visit. *To buy a present for your cousin. Nothing for us. Remember? We would not be buying the unicorn today.*

Through big, teary eyes, Dahlia watched me put the unicorn back on the shelf. As we walked away she became so distraught, she started to wail. And the further we got from the unicorn, the louder she wailed. Inside, I was dying a slow death. But I'd said no, and I was NOT going to give in. If I did, I knew this scenario would be repeated every time we went into a store—possibly for the rest of our lives. I pictured a teenage version of my sweet Dahlia, screaming at me to buy her the new hoodie she'd spotted in the window of Abercrombie and Fitch.

I held my ground.

"I'm sorry, Dahlia, but we're not buying the unicorn today. Put him on your wish list and you might get him for a birthday, Christmas, or Hanukkah present. But not today, okay honey?"

The wailing just got louder. I grabbed my niece's book off the shelf and raced to the cash register, towing Dahlia behind me and silently cursing myself for not saving this errand for another time. All the while, strangers started coming up to us, trying their best to soothe the sobbing child attached to my hand. Cookies, gum, crayons— anything they could find in their purses or pockets to stop the crying. I did my best to politely decline over the ear-splitting moans of my unicorn-deprived daughter. "No, thank you. You're very kind, but *no*."

Clearly the strangers hadn't learned the "no means no" lesson from their parents because they wouldn't give up. As we hurried past the coffee shop, the barista chased after us with a handful of biscotti for Dahlia. No joke. Somehow, I made it to the cash register and out of the store without caving and going back for the stupid unicorn. But it was hard. Yup, saying no to your children can sometimes be *really* hard. But I promise it will make them grow up stronger. And, ultimately, it will make your job as a parent easier when they figure out they can always take you at your word—and that when you say no, you mean it.

Answer her questions

Children learn by watching, mimicking their elders, and asking questions. As every parent of young children knows, kids LOVE to ask questions. So many questions, it can make even the most patient parent want to invest in a good pair of ear plugs. Of course, asking questions is vital to your child's understanding of the world. At this age, you'll notice that your Money Baby's questions are becoming more detailed and complex than ever before.

And in return, she deserves thoughtful, informed answers to these questions.

Deborah writes: At five years old, our precocious daughter Dahlia did something that caught me off guard. She began asking her father and me an endless stream of questions about our family's finances. "How much does our house cost?" "How much do you pay the handyman?" "The cleaning lady?" "The car mechanic?" "How much money do you make?" "How much did our last vacation cost?"

At first, I was floored by these questions. How and why would it occur to someone so young to be asking us these things? Shouldn't she be thinking about toys and naps and teddy bears? Her older brother had never once questioned us about money and finances.

My next thought was a selfish one. Understanding a little bit about kids at this point and knowing that five-year-olds aren't exactly the most discreet individuals on the planet, I worried Dahlia would start telling her friends all the intimate details about our family's finances. Did I really want the whole neighbourhood knowing how much we earn and what we paid for our house?

Definitely not.

As Dahlia smiled up at me, patiently waiting for my answer, I made a hasty decision—a bad decision, as it turns out. I told her these things were "private" and "grown-up concerns" and she could worry about them when she was older.

Yup, big mistake.

Through the process of researching this book, I've come to realize that these were actually very mature questions and that her interest in our family's finances at such a young age was something to be encouraged ... not squelched. As I said before, we all make mistakes. And luckily, I still had lots of time to change my tune. Now Dahlia is six years old and, thankfully, she's still asking questions. I answer them all to the best of my ability.

The bottom line is this: don't shy away from the hard questions. If your child is old enough to ask, she's old enough for a thoughtful answer. Remember, at this age your Money Baby will still have some difficulty understanding any explanation that's too complex, so it's important to use clear, simple, age-appropriate terms.

Of course, understanding more about finances will serve your Money Baby well in the future. Maybe with a bit of encouragement (and the lessons from this book) she'll grow up to be the next Warren Buffett.

Wouldn't that be nice?

Remember, children of all ages need patience, support and encouragement. Money management is a difficult subject to tackle—even for many adults—and having the freedom to make mistakes is essential. Better your children make mistakes now, when the stakes are still low, than lose the farm when they're adults because they didn't know any better.

MAKING IT FUN
Books

It goes without saying that children of this age love being read to. Here are a few age-appropriate picture books you can read to your Money Babies to help them get interested in the topic and start the discussion going in your home.

The Berenstain Bears' Dollars and Sense by Stan and Jan Berenstain. Warning: don't read this book to the kids unless you are willing and ready to talk about the idea of an allowance with them. The story revolves around the decision by the Bear parents to give the cubs an allowance and how the young ones immediately rush out, spend it all, and then sulk because they don't have any more money. Momma Bear comes up with an idea to encourage the cubs to give more thought to what they want to buy and spend their allowance more carefully. We're rather dubious about her method but, hey—she's a bear. Like all Berenstain Bear books, the kids will probably love it.

Benny's Pennies by Pat Brisson. This is a short rhyming story about a boy who spends his five new pennies buying little things to make his family happy—a rose for his mother, a cookie for his brother, a paper hat for his sister, a bone for his dog, and a fish for his cat. Okay, so the prices of these items aren't realistic, and there's no mention of Benny saving any of his pennies in his piggy bank, but these aren't the points of the book. Instead, the story demonstrates how we use money to buy things and imparts a message of selflessness and smart spending. Benny doesn't waste his money frivolously … he sets out with a shopping list in mind and puts his pennies to good use. It's a nice book to enjoy with your Money Baby. What would *you* buy with five pennies?

Bunny Money by Rosemary Wells. Children who are familiar with the popular cartoon rabbits, Max and Ruby, will enjoy this tale of the pair setting off to buy a birthday present for their Grandma. After listening to the story of how Max and Ruby ran out of money during their adventure, our Money Baby decided the rabbit siblings should have stayed focused on the goal of their shopping expedition instead of wasting their money on things they didn't really need (like candy teeth and cupcakes). If a six-year-old can pick up a lesson like that from an eight-dollar book, it's money well spent in our opinion.

One Cent, Two Cents, Old Cent, New Cent: All About Money (Cat in the Hat's Learning Library) by Bonnie Worth. This is a fun book told in rhyme with colourful illustrations starring the familiar characters from Dr. Seuss's *The Cat in the Hat*. There's lots of interesting information here about the history of money, rare coins, and an explanation of how the minting process works. Unfortunately, the final part of the book is geared exclusively to an American audience. Our Canadian Money Babies were left a bit confused by the images of Abraham Lincoln and Benjamin Franklin in the place of Queen Elizabeth on the illustrated coins. If you don't mind pausing the story to explain about the difference between American and Canadian money, it's a worthwhile book.

Fun with coins

Piggy bank. If she doesn't have one already, this is the perfect age for your Money Baby to receive his first piggy bank. There are "design-your-own" type banks that kids can paint, colour, and decorate. Or choose a bank that's transparent or visually interesting in some other way. Some banks have elaborate mechanisms that allow a coin to tumble and slide before settling to the bottom. Many children are enthralled with the process and will spend quite a while watching the coins fall. The more interesting the bank, the more excited the kids will be about the idea of saving money.

Birthdate coins. Explain to your Money Babies how every coin has a date stamped onto it. Now empty out a jar of coins onto a table and see if they can find a penny with their birth year on it. Follow with nickels, dimes, quarters, loonies, and toonies. They'll be proud of themselves when this little game is done.

Coin rubbing art project. Gather coins of all denominations and place them (queen-side down) on a table with a piece of white paper firmly on top. Using the lead side of a pencil (not the tip) or the side of a peeled crayon, gently rub until the impression of the coin comes through. See if your child can identify the coin by the picture that appears, then lift the paper to see if she's right.

Store. This is a variation of the exercise described earlier. Give the child some coins or play money. Set your "prices" on various items in easy-to-add denominations and take turns being the cashier. This is a good opportunity to demonstrate how to double-check a bill before handing over your money. When it's your turn to be the cashier, "accidently" slip in an extra charge and see if she catches you.

Cash register. If you don't already have a toy cash register, you might want to consider buying one. Or, better yet, borrow one from a friend with older children. With their big buttons and ringing sounds, toy cash registers are always a favourite with children, and this is the perfect time to let your Money Baby start using one.

On-line games

There are lots of on-line money games that your Money Baby might enjoy. However, choose carefully—some may be too advanced for this age while others are not appropriate for Canadian kids, such as those games offered on the U.S. Mint website which, of course, focus on American coins, U.S. states, and presidents. Here are a few that are worth a look.

Money Metropolis. You'll find this at www.practical moneyskills.com. Click on the Games tab but turn the speaker on your computer down first—the background music comes booming out (happily it stops once the game begins).

The first step is to create a player by choosing a boy or girl, giving him/her a name, and then selecting colours for skin, hair, and clothing. Click "Play," and your character is ready to start.

We created a little girl named Susie for our trial. Susie was asked to begin by deciding what she wants to save for.

The options include a zoo party ($200), a pet dog ($300), and a plane trip ($400). Once that's decided, a map of Susie's town appears. Move the cursor around the map to take Susie to the places she (actually your Money Baby) wants to visit. The choices include a grocery store, clothing store, library, general store, gas station, news stand, arcade, and various homes. Susie starts the game with her monthly allowance, which is $40.

Each place she visits offers an opportunity to make or spend money. At the filling station, she can get a job pumping gas—not something a six-year-old would do in the real world, but hey, it's only a game. Susie has to fill twenty gas tanks within the allotted time to earn $10. If she isn't fast enough, she gets nothing. We couldn't do it, but your child may have more dexterity.

Next we took Susie to Caroline's house where the job was to mow a lawn for $10. But if the lawn mower bumps into too many trees or bushes, Susie gets nothing.

Frustrated by her unsuccessful attempts to earn cash, Susie headed for Nora's Arcade where she blew $5 playing games. Then she headed over to the library where she got a job sorting books alphabetically. She aced that one and earned $10, so she was feeling pretty good again. She wandered over to Mae's house where a babysitting job earned her another $15. She was on a roll!

You get the idea. The kids have fun moving their character around the town and trying to earn money along the way. They may have to go to the General Store occasionally to buy something they need for a job, such as a bike or a rake. They can check how much money they have at any time by clicking on the "Your Budget" tab. The game ends when the savings goal is reached.

This is a good way to learn about saving, earning, and spending money, and the visuals, while basic, are colourful and amusing. Your child will enjoy it.

There are several other games on this website but those that are appropriate for this age group use American coins, which may be confusing for your child. The others are for older kids.

Change Maker. This can be found at www.funbrain. com/cashreg. This is a great way for your child to learn about making change, although you may need to help out, at least at the start. Unlike most on-line coin-counting games that we found, this one offers a Canadian currency option (also United States, Mexico, Australia, and the United Kingdom, if you plan to go travelling). There are four levels of difficulty, ranging from Easy to Super Brain. Start with Easy.

The game itself is very simple and is like visiting a store. The child has made a purchase, let's say of 47 cents, and has paid $1. The challenge is to figure out how much change she is due. Click on the Canadian coins displayed (from 1 cent to $2) to enter the correct answer. A counter keeps the running score.

The Hard level adds $5, $10, and $20 bills to the mix while $50s and $100s appear at the Super Brain level. If you have a mathematical whiz on your hands, she might be able to handle that one (what's $50 minus $25.95?), but don't push beyond her limits. This is supposed to be fun.

Money Master. Go to www.mathisfun.com. There are sixteen currency options to choose from; select the Canadian one. There are eight skill levels from which to choose so start at the easiest and work up. The game itself is very simple—just move the coins so as to reach a target amount. You get a point for each successful try.

Apps

Kid Review: Learning Money With Leo (app for iPad)

Sponsor: Royal Bank

Comments: This app is really fun because it teaches you more about money, like how to save it and spend it in a smart way. There's a game where you have to buy your own stickers and a read-along story about two kids who have to earn money to buy something for their dog.

Strong points: The piggy bank game was really good because it taught me which coins are which and how to sort them. I played this a lot.

Weak points: I liked the colouring game, but it really didn't have anything to do with money.

Favourite feature: The maze game was my favourite—you have to roll the coin through the maze to get it to its match. I also like the spot-the-difference game.

Rating: 5/5

Reviewer: Dahlia, age six

SUMMING UP

This is a critical age in teaching children about money. It's the time for putting in place a solid foundation that can be built on as the years go by—how to count, the value of coins, shopping, and basic budgeting. Once your kids have mastered these fundamentals, you'll be ready to move to the next stage.

This is also the time to ensure your kids understand that they cannot have everything they want. It's one of the most important financial lessons you can teach them.

3
CONSUMERS IN TRAINING—AGES 7-8

I'm saving up for a BlackBerry.
—LILY, AGE EIGHT

GETTING READY

With the kindergarten years squarely behind him, your school-age child is now ready to take on more responsibility and tackle increasingly difficult concepts and complex problems. Seven- and eight-year-olds enjoy figuring out the world with the use of role-playing and "staged learning." They like taking some risks and upping the level of difficulty for all the tasks in life. This is also the stage where children like to share, trade, collect, and compare themselves to their peers. Yes, your little Money Baby has now grown into a Consumer in Training.

By the end of grade one, he's mastered counting, measuring, simple addition, and subtraction. By the end of grade two, he may also be able to understand basic fractions. You'll find he enjoys being challenged, working hard, and completing tasks. He takes great pride in his accomplishments and loves getting "jobs" to do that help show off his growing independence. (Note to parents: enjoy this stage now because it doesn't last long!)

. . . .

Two quarters or a dollar bill?

A young boy goes into the local convenience store. The owner spots him and whispers to a customer, "This is the stupidest kid ever. Watch this. I'll prove it."

He reaches into the till and pulls out some coins. He calls the boy over and holds out two hands. In one, there's a loonie. In the other, two quarters. "You choose which hand you want, son," the owner says.

The boy takes the quarters, thanks the owner, and leaves. The man turns back to the customer. "What did I tell you?" he says. "His parents never taught that kid to count!"

A few minutes later, the customer leaves and sees the boy coming out of an ice cream store across the street. He goes up to the kid and says, "Hey, son! May I ask you a question? Why did you take the quarters instead of the loonie?"

The boy licks his cone and replies: "Because the day I take the loonie, the game's over!"

. . . .

All of this means that, developmentally, he's ready for the next stage of his financial education.

At this age, kids usually have a pretty solid concept of money and what it's used for. Now is the time to start teaching them the basics of how to prioritize spending and saving. An allowance can be a very good way to do this. Yes, parents—loosen up those wallets because this is the stage where allowances generally begin. According to a random sample of Canadian parents with children eighteen or older conducted by Environics Research Group for CIBC (Canadian Imperial Bank of Commerce), the average age at which Canadian parents begin to give their child an allowance is seven.

Remember, children of this age will still be asking lots of questions and watching you closely for clues on how to handle situations. So parents, if you want your child to grow up with strong financial instincts, it's important to practise what you preach. Let them see you making smart financial decisions in your own life and keeping your impulse buys to a minimum.

HOW-TO
Let's go shopping

Fortunately for parents, taking your child to a store isn't the chore it used to be when they were toddlers. They're much less needy and uncertain now and instead are curious and enthusiastic when faced with new things. Add in the fact that their attention span is better than ever before and it makes sense that most seven- and eight-year-olds are a delight to bring to the store.

So let's talk about shopping.

As we mentioned, your school-age child is ready to tackle increasingly difficult challenges. So now that your

Consumer in Training has learned how to identify money and has had a lesson at the dollar store, it's time to take it up a notch. This is the right age for him to master how to count money and make change.

If you haven't already done so, it's time to explain the concept that money is based on the dollar ... that coins are fractions of dollars and bills are multiples of dollars. Explain about equivalents and show him how four quarters, ten dimes, twenty nickels, or a hundred pennies all equal one dollar. With a small number of coins and bills in front of him, give him some practice scenarios and see if he can figure out which combination of coins and bills he can offer for payment.

Remember to make the point that, when paying for something, he either has to offer the exact amount or something that exceeds it and then ask for change. In this age of credit and debit cards, knowing how to count and make change is a lesson that is often overlooked by parents and caregivers. Don't fool yourself into thinking it's not important. That's like deciding not to teach your children to tie their shoes because of the prevalence of Velcro fasteners. Or not teaching them how to print because "everyone texts and types these days." Understanding how to make change is a life skill that every child should master.

Figuring out how much change you're owed on a purchase in real life means doing calculations in your head, as paper and pencils aren't readily available at checkout lines. Of course, most registers will show the amount of change due, but your child should be able to do the calculation himself so he can be sure it is correct and that he has not been overcharged.

This is something that your children will have to practise quite a bit before they get it right. Since addition is usually easier for young children than subtraction, the simplest way for them to learn how to make change is to count forward from the price of the item to the amount they will tender. For example, if the item he wants to buy costs eighty-seven cents and he has paid one dollar, he should count forward from eighty-seven cents to figure out how much change is owed to him. When starting out, break this down into tiny steps that will be easy for him to understand. Count out loud with pennies as you're counting up (eighty-eight, eighty-nine, ninety) then see if he can tell you which coin will make the amount jump from ninety to one hundred. If he gets it right, start over again with a different set of numbers.

If your child enjoys learning on a computer, there are several fun websites where he can practise these skills, such as www.funbrain.com/cashreg/index.html and www.mathisfun.com/money/money-master.html. We like these because they offer a Canadian currency option. You'll find detailed reviews in Chapter 2.

Double-checking

Help to get your children into the habit of counting the change they're given at a store. Not only will it sharpen their math skills, it's a good habit that might save them from costly mistakes during their lives.

Introducing tax

Yes, your Consumer in Training is still very young, but before that trip to the store you need to introduce him to the concept of sales tax. This means explaining to him that the price marked on the shelf is not what he's going to actually pay when he reaches the check-out counter.

You can be sure that he's not going to like the idea very much—but then, who does? Moreover, it is going to complicate your making change lessons. That item that costs eighty-seven cents based on the shelf price will actually cost anywhere from ninety-one cents in Alberta, where only the 5 percent GST applies, to one dollar in Nova Scotia, where the combined GST and provincial sales tax is 15 percent. So if he pays one dollar in Alberta, he'll receive nine cents in change, whereas in Nova Scotia he'd get nothing back.

Unless he is a mathematical genius, he is not going to be able to do those calculations in his head. So you may want to consider showing him how to do them on a pocket calculator (you may have one as an app on your cellphone).

All right, after lots of practising at home, it's time to take him to the real store and let him make a purchase on his own (of course, with you standing by to help if necessary, calculator in hand).

Want versus need

At this age, your Consumer in Training is old enough to start learning how to prioritize. Understanding the difference between "want" and "need" at an early age is crucial and could have a huge impact on your child's spending habits later in life. When you consider the fact that Canadian household debt levels are at record highs, it's clear that this is a lesson many adults of today would have benefited from in childhood.

Debt crisis

A TransUnion study suggests Canadian debt loads grew at an average 4.5 percent in the first quarter of 2011 compared to a year earlier. The credit bureau's analysis found that total debt per consumer, excluding mortgages, grew to $25,597 in the first three months of 2011, up from $24,497 in the same quarter of 2010.

Indeed, kids who don't understand the difference between "want" and "need" are at risk of developing a mindset of perpetual craving and dissatisfaction. Let's start this generation off on the right foot and get them properly prepared. There are endless ways you can choose to illustrate the difference between "want" and "need." Perhaps the best place to start the discussion is in your child's bedroom.

As parents know, the amount of stuff an average Canadian kid accumulates in a given year can be mindblowing. New clothes, shoes, books, birthday gifts, arts and crafts projects, loot bags, presents from Grandma … all of it inevitably brought home and dumped in his room. When he's really young, keeping a child's room pared down is a never-ending challenge for parents. But as he grows, getting your child involved in the "spring cleaning" process is important, beyond the basics of hygiene and organization.

Look around your child's room with him by your side and see how he answers the following questions: What are the things in here you *need*? (A bed to sleep in, a desk for homework, clothes to wear, etc.). And what are the things in here you *want*? (Toys, books, games, stuffed animals, etc).

Once the difference has been established, ask your child what he's ready to part with from the "want" group. Using separate bags for garbage, recycling, and charity, sort through the room together and help him figure out what items it's time to give up.

Broken? Into the garbage or recycling.

Unused? Into a charity box.

Some choices will be easy (outgrown clothes, toys that are too babyish, books he's practically committed to memory). But other choices will be more difficult and some partings more sentimental. Just remember, herein lies your child's first lessons about how to make tough decisions, prioritize, and pass on the stuff that's not important to him. These lessons will serve him well in his life. Learning how to get by with less will not only set your child onto the right road for financial management, it might keep him from being the subject of a future episode of *Hoarders*.

Outside the house, there are even more ways to teach this lesson. Even a simple trip to the grocery store can help illustrate the difference between "want" and "need." What are the things we "need" to buy? (Food to nourish our bodies and keep us healthy and fit.) What is the stuff we "want" to buy? (Food that satisfies our cravings but provides no nutritional benefit.)

Turn it into a game and see if he can point out the difference between the "need" foods and the "wants" (hint, most of the "wants" will be located in the middle aisles of the store). Of course, it's okay to have some things in life that we don't necessarily need. We all like to indulge in some "wants" once in a while. But learning how to distinguish between these two things could be one of the most important financial lessons you can impart to your child. People who know how to "want what they have" are the ones who are much more likely to live within their means.

Allowance

Of course, to really understand about spending and saving your child will need some money with which to practise … otherwise known as an allowance.

It's a fact that seven- and eight-year-old children benefit greatly from "staged learning"—in other words, acting things out in a safe environment is a good way for them to better understand the world around them. With this in mind, instead of you just explaining money to him, this is your child's chance to "act it out" by having some of his own to spend. Consider an allowance as role playing for the real world of finance.

For these reasons, we recommend giving your child an allowance. Would you let your child drive a car by himself down the highway if he hadn't had lessons and months, perhaps years, of practice? No, you wouldn't. But you can get through life without ever knowing how to drive a car. Unless you're living deep in the mountains of a remote Pacific island, you can't, however, get through life without using money. Learning how to use it wisely will take practice. And an allowance is exactly that.

If you decide that an allowance is the way you want to go, you'll need to come up with a plan that suits your family. Here are a few questions you'll have to ask yourself before you start. Remember, there are no right and wrong answers. It's up to every parent to determine the system that works best for them. Here are some points to consider.

When is the best time to start giving your child an allowance? As mentioned earlier, most Canadian families start offering their children an allowance at age seven. We like the idea of starting at this age for exactly the same reasons we've named this stage "Consumers in Training." Your child is out of kindergarten and into grade school. He is ready to be challenged by more complex problems and has moved beyond simple math skills. In other words, this is the perfect age to start real-life lessons about saving and spending.

How much should you give him? Opinions vary on this and, of course, the final say will be up to each family. Starting out, many parents offer their kids one dollar per year of age. Some offer one dollar per grade in school. Some families take the simple route and hand over five dollars to each child, regardless of age or grade level. However much you give them, just make sure it's enough for them to really experiment with. Remember the purpose of an allowance is to give your child hands-on practice with money. He'll have a hard time learning anything if he doesn't have enough to experiment with (and yes, make mistakes).

● ●

Kid quote

If you don't have a lot of money, you can be poor, so make sure you have some money.—Eden, age seven

● ●

Part of determining the allowance amount will depend on what your child will be responsible to pay for with this money. Is the allowance to be used simply for "treat money" (candy, comic books, and popsicles)? Or will your child now be expected to pay for gifts for family and friends, transportation, school supplies, books, toys, clothes, McDonalds?

At the Consumer in Training stage, we recommend a small amount to be used for treats and little indulgences. As he gets older and the allowance increases, he can start to take on more responsibility for his own expenses.

How often should you give the allowance? Once a week? Once a month? Whenever you remember?

It's a good idea to have a set payment schedule when it comes to an allowance. After all, that's the way the real world works. Offering a weekly allowance is a good idea as it's frequent, consistent, and will quickly become part of your family's routine. Choose a day that works best for you, keeping in mind that kids have the most opportunity to spend money over the weekends. If you want their allowances to stretch out over a full week, consider giving it on a Sunday. But definitely set up some kind of payment system that will make it easy for you to remember. (Of course, if you forget, your child will almost certainly remind you.)

Should you tie their allowance to chores or will it be given freely? We encourage you not to tie allowances to household chores. Helping out around the house is a responsibility that every member of the household should carry, without expectation of financial reimbursement. Parents work around the house (taking out the garbage, cooking meals, doing the laundry, etc.) without payment and so should your child (jobs should be allocated at age-appropriate levels, naturally).

Caroline Munshaw agrees with this point—she's one of the co-founders of Cent$ible Students, a program created to further financial literacy education for Canadian elementary school students (www.centsiblestudents.ca).

"We do not tie household chores to allowance," she says. "However, chores are still important. Everyone is expected to complete age-appropriate tasks to contribute to the household. If these chores are not completed, (children) will not lose their allowance, but they may lose TV time! In this scenario, there certainly is still a relationship between work and money—underscore that *you*, the parent, work *hard* for money, but the child is a working member of the family and is receiving a part of this income. What comes with it is responsibility, a list of expectations that are to be determined by you—perhaps with some buy in or discussion with your child—as to what chores need to be done around the house."

Once it becomes a habit, your child's participation in the upkeep of the household will become a source of pride and will reaffirm his role in the family unit. If you tie an allowance to chores, you're not teaching anything about co-operation. What will happen down the line, when your child grows into a teenager and has an independent source of income (like babysitting, a paper route, or a part-time job) and no longer needs an allowance? If allowance and chores have always gone hand-in-hand, you'll probably find your teenager scoffing at the idea of helping out in the home the second he's too "rich" to bother.

It's best to start this habit when your kids are still in their "I want to help" stage. In Deborah's home, the number of responsibilities her children have directly corresponds to their age. At the time of writing, Dahlia was six and therefore had six jobs she was responsible for daily:

Keeping her room clean
Making her bed
Feeding her fish
Completing homework
Practising piano
Dustbusting the floor

Jonah, at nine years old, had nine daily jobs:

Keeping his room clean
Making his bed
Feeding his fish
Completing homework
Practising piano
Setting the table
Mentoring an emerging reader (i.e., reading with his
    sister)
Emptying the dishwasher
Clearing the table

What about extras? Some families offer an extra sum of money for larger jobs that are out of the realm of a child's everyday responsibilities. In most cases, this would be something you'd find yourself paying an outsider to do if you weren't doing it yourself (for example, yard work, shovelling the driveway, weeding the garden, babysitting a younger sibling).

No more handouts. Once you and your partner have committed to the idea of an allowance, you must also commit to putting a moratorium on handouts. An allowance is your children's way to learn how to budget, save, and handle money. If you continually step in to supply more, what lesson are you really teaching them? Simply that handouts will always come if they've spent the allowance money and want something else. If that's the lesson they get from an allowance, then they're *really* in for a rude awakening when they're out in the real world.

Bite your tongue. Remember, the purpose of giving your children an allowance is to help them learn about money management at an early age. You won't be doing your child any favours if you're standing over him and telling him how to spend his cash. As with all other aspects of life, making mistakes is an important part of the learning process. Your child had to fall down many times before he learned how to walk. So let him fall down and make some mistakes with his money ... better now when the stakes are still relatively low.

Ready, set, go! Once you've decided on an amount and a schedule for your child's allowance, it's time to put a few measures in place so he can easily manage his money and learn best from the experience. Of course, you could give your children total control over how they choose to spend their money. But for an allowance to pack the most educational punch, we think it's a good idea to offer some guidance. You might have heard it suggested that you give your kids three separate banks: one for spending, one for saving, and one for sharing. If not, you're about to hear it now. Whether it's jars, banks, boxes, or Tupperware containers, they will all serve the goal of physically and visually dividing up your children's money so they understand that it's not all for spending.

Virtual banking

For those who prefer using "virtual money," there are several websites that can help you and your children track their spending and saving. It's important to note that with all of these sites, no actual money is involved. The sites offer an easy and convenient way to keep track of all the numbers for you. When your child asks for actual money, you adjust the on-line numbers accordingly.

There are plenty of these websites to choose from. Here are some places to start:

KidsAllowanceBank: http://kidsallowancebank.com
Zefty: http://zefty.com
ThreeJars: www.threejars.com/home
FamilyMint: http://familymint.com
MoneyTrail: www.moneytrail.net
Bankaroo: www.bankaroo.com/home

All of these sites act as an imaginary bank, with you (the parents) as the tellers. Using on-line tools like these, you and your child can keep track of your children's finances from your computer. Some of them offer an automatic deposit (which adds the preset allowance to your child's "account" at the rate you've preselected). We like this feature as it eliminates the stress of having to remember every week and running out to get exact change for their piggy banks. All of these sites also mimic the real-life experience of banking, which ups the learning quotient. Some of these are accessible through mobile devices. Some link allowance to chores. Some allow you to divide the funds into separate categories for spending, saving, and sharing. Some are free (which we like). Others offer more bells and whistles, but are only available for a fee (albeit a relatively low one).

FirstKidBank.com is one of our favourites as it lets you keep track of your child's spending from your mobile phone (great for when you're out shopping with your child and the piggy bank is at home). There are ways to set up separate accounts for spending, saving, and sharing. As well, there is a "chore" section that allows you to keep track of payment for extra jobs. Best of all, it's free!

DEBORAH'S STORY OF JONAH AND THE SLUSHIE

As I mentioned in Chapter 2, I had been debating whether or not to offer my own children an allowance. The answer, I promised them, would come by the time I finished writing this book.

In the meantime, we had a money problem brewing with our oldest child. It all started with a one-time treat—a Slushie to celebrate the end of the school year. Jonah had graduated from grade two, Dahlia from junior kindergarten, and I wanted to buy them a little treat to mark the occasion. They were thrilled with their icy, sugary trophies. And that was that. Or so I thought.

By the time spring rolled around the next year, the "treat" had morphed into a regular Friday afternoon request to "celebrate the end of the school week." Pretty soon, it grew into a daily after-school plea. Every day when I'd pick him up, Jonah would beg "can we go to Mac's Milk and get a Slushie?"

He'd come up with every excuse possible.

"I did well on a test." "It's a hot day." "They've come up with a new flavour."

Usually, I'd say no. But every now and then, on a really hot day, there'd be a yes. Powered by these little crumbs of encouragement, my brilliantly innovative child began coming up with new angles every single day. Before long, the daily battle over a Slushie began to get exhausting. I didn't want to be the kind of parent who wouldn't indulge her kids in the occasional inexpensive treat but this was just too much.

I tried explaining to Jonah how money is a finite commodity and how the financial choices we make (even the small ones) determine how much of it we have. How spending two dollars on a Slushie may not seem like a lot of money, but if I were to buy him and his sister one every day for a year (like he was asking for) it would add up to over $1,200. He looked pained, shuffling his feet and sighing throughout my diatribe. Regardless of what I said, his mind was fixated on that Slushie. Wising up, I stopped bringing my wallet with me when I picked up the kids from school. This put an end to the Slushie appeals, although my son's sulky faces and dramatic sighs let me know he was disappointed. Finally, it occurred to me that if he was spending his own money, he might not be so Slushie-obsessed. Yes, it's always so much easier to spend someone else's money, isn't it? I began thinking an allowance might be a good way to handle the situation. Soon after that, I started research on this book.

It wasn't long into the writing process before I figured out what the answer was.

Deborah's Allowance Answer: I now understand the importance of giving your children an allowance. We've started offering each of our children one dollar for each grade. Jonah gets four dollars and Dahlia will receive two dollars per week when she turns seven (in grade two). If he desperately wants that Slushie, now he can use his own money.

LEARNING TO SAVE

It's easy to persuade young children to save when they don't know the value of money. Just give them a piggy bank and encourage them to drop coins into it. Since they don't know that coins can be used for anything else at that stage, they'll do it happily.

But once they learn that those coins can be exchanged for things they want, the whole dynamic changes. Now you're asking them to exchange immediate gratification for a longer term benefit. If it's not clear just what that benefit is, you may have a fight on your hands.

Saving is one of the most important lessons you can teach your kids because, if the habit is established early, it will last a lifetime—and may keep your children from financial disaster when they reach adulthood.

Author David Chilton's two *Wealthy Barber* bestsellers are both based on the central theme of "Pay yourself first"— in other words, save a portion of your income before you commit to spending a penny.

Grown-ups have no problem identifying savings goals: a new car, a down payment on a house, a retirement plan, college education for the kids, and more. The difficulty is finding the money to put aside. There never seems to be enough, with household budgets stretched to the limit. If the savings habit did not become deeply engrained from an early age, the willpower to make it happen may not be there. That's part of the reason why household debt levels have risen to record levels in recent years.

Children, fortunately, are in a better situation. They don't have tight budgets to deal with. Putting food on the table and keeping the roof in good repair are not on their priority list. So, ironically, they are actually in a better position to save than their parents.

The trick is to make them *want* to do it. The only way to achieve that is by holding out the prospect of a reward at the end of the process.

Now that they have an allowance, that should be fairly easy. If you follow our advice, the granting of an allowance will come with the stipulation that there will be no more handouts. If you can't buy it with your own money, you can't have it. Sorry, but those are the rules.

Now, for the first time, the child is faced with a decision. Does he run to the store and shoot the works on candy bars and Slushies? Or does he save some of that money for something he wants more?

. . . .

Gordon's books

My grandchildren find this hard to believe, but when I was a boy not only were there no computers, but there was no television either. So my great passion became reading. At an early age, I became enthralled with the Oz books when my mother read them to me, and by the age of five or six I was able to read them myself.

During those years, my parents bought me all the books I wanted. But at about age eight, I received a Hardy Boys book called *The Mystery of Cabin Island* as a Christmas gift. I devoured it in less than a day and in the process discovered there was a whole series just waiting for me. I begged my mother to buy more but she wasn't thrilled with them—she felt they were trashy and wanted me to read more literary works.

I was able to borrow a few Hardy Boys books from the school library, but their collection was small and most of them were lent out. My only other option was to buy them myself—in those days they cost $1.99 each, which to me was a small fortune.

That's when I started saving in earnest. I really, *really* wanted those books—more than I wanted chocolate sodas, which was saying a lot at the time. I didn't get an allowance, but I did receive a quarter for cutting the lawn (which was about half an acre in size) and for other chores. It was also about that time that I began to earn some money for delivering telegrams in the neighbourhood. It all went into my piggy bank, which fortunately came with a removable plug in the bottom so I could get at coins without using a hammer.

When I had saved enough, I gave it to my mother and asked her to order the books I wanted from the Sears Roebuck catalogue. Although she didn't approve of my choice of reading material, she did like the idea that I had learned to save and went along with the plan. For two weeks after the order was sent, I would haunt the mailbox waiting for the books to arrive.

I gave up a lot of sodas and ice creams to save for those books. But the reward was well worth it.

• •

Help your child with the decision. Talk about what's most important to him. Make him understand that if he wants that video game, he is going to have to save for it out of his allowance. If he doesn't, then he will never get it.

Encourage him to begin saving for something that is not too expensive. If gratification is delayed for too long at the beginning, your child may decide it's hopeless and lose interest, so try to get him to focus on a goal that can be reached within a month. The satisfaction he will feel when he reaches it will encourage him to continue the savings habit—hopefully, for life.

Sadly, the idea of waiting, economizing, and saving your pennies until you can actually afford to pay for something has become old-fashioned. Let's revive it for the next generation and help to keep our children from running into the same debt crisis our credit-card generation has created for itself.

SHARING THE WEALTH

If your child is now receiving an allowance and earmarking a portion of it for charity, it's time to help him understand what that really means. This is an integral step in truly comprehending the value of money—not just what you can buy for yourself, but how you can use it to help others.

Young children are notoriously egocentric. Although they innately have great capacity for compassion, it's quite natural for them to see themselves as the centre of the world. By age seven, however, things are starting to change. Now children are mature enough to be able to appreciate viewpoints that are different from their own. At this age, your child is capable of thinking rationally and ethically. If you haven't already, this is a good time to introduce the idea of charity.

How many times have you heard your child wail *"it's not fair"*? Unless you're raising your children in an igloo, it's probably more than a googolplex (Deborah's kids' favourite number). In our homes, the answer to this complaint is simply and consistently: "No, it's not. But the world isn't fair."

And it's not. How is it fair that some children grow up with food, shelter, loving parents, education, and health care, while others have none? No, the world isn't a fair place. And you're not doing your child any favours by pretending it is. But now that he's reached the age where he's capable of understanding this, it's time to show him how he can help.

In our society, we often think of charity as "giving." In Hebrew, the word for charity is *tzedekah,* which translates to mean "justice." Thinking of it this way puts a completely different spin on the concept. Justice denotes a certain responsibility that children, who seem to live in a perpetual quest for fairness, can really understand. Watch your children's faces as you serve each a piece of cake or a bowl of ice cream. If there's even a sliver of difference in size, they'll know. We've actually watched our kids count the number of chocolate chips in their cookies to see who got more. Even though they know what the answer will be, they still try to suggest it isn't fair. And maybe it's not. No, the world isn't fair. And so we share what we have to help make it more so for the people around the world who aren't as fortunate as us. That's the notion of justice.

You probably spent a good part of the toddler years teaching your child how to share toys. Now, it's time to explain how sharing works on a greater scale. And how they can start contributing with their own money.

If you give your kids an allowance, the amount that goes into the sharing bank is something you'll have to figure out for your own family. We recommend 10 percent. That's not so much that there won't be anything left over for them to learn about spending and saving. And 10 percent will add up over the year. If you give your child five dollars a week, by the end of the year he'll have $26 to donate to a charity of his choice. That's a significant monetary contribution for a young child to make.

Where to donate the money should be a decision your child is involved with. Perhaps there's a charity that has particular significance to your family. Or maybe there's a local charitable initiative in your community. Deborah found that, when teaching her kids about charity, giving to one that helps other children was especially significant and something her own kids could relate to. So they donate to the SickKids Foundation as well as Creation of Hope, a charity that directly funds orphaned children of Kikima, Kenya. But there are lots of worthy organizations from which to choose.

If your child doesn't receive an allowance, there are still opportunities for him to donate money to charity. If your child is on board with this decision, he can ask for donations in lieu of presents for his next birthday party. (Make the suggestion, but don't be disappointed if he decides against this, though … it's asking a lot of a kid.) If he likes the idea of giving to a charity but isn't quite ready to give up all his gifts, there are ways he can do both. On-line birthday sites like Echoage will send out your party invitations and set it up so that your guests can contribute money instead of gifts. When the party's over, half the money collected will go the charity of your child's choice. There's a long list of charities that have partnered with this site including

Autism Speaks Canada, Make a Wish Foundation, and Boys and Girls Clubs of Canada. Your child receives the second half of the collected money with which to purchase a gift of his choice. You can find out more at www.echoage.com.

Remember, donating gifts and money should be something your child feels enthusiastic about and involved with. If he's feeling forced to give, the lesson will be completely lost. Starting young will help develop a habit of sharing that will hopefully last him a lifetime.

CAITLIN'S CHRISTMAS

Several years ago, we wrote a Christmas trivia book entitled *Quizmas*. We also created a Quizmas website at www.quizmas.ca and invited people to submit their Christmas memories. One that we published came from Leesa Seaward of Halifax, Nova Scotia, who told us the inspirational story of her daughter, Caitlin, and sharing.

When Caitlin was eight years old, she remarked as she and her mom were putting away the Christmas gifts that everyone had received too much and that the money should be used to "buy gifts for unfortunate people." Her parents initially dismissed it as an off-hand remark, but the following year as the malls started their holiday decorating, Caitlin reiterated it. Her parents agreed and started to hold family meetings and make lists of charities they all wanted to donate to. Caitlin's priorities included visiting war veterans in the local Veteran's Hospital; donating money, clothes and toys to a women's and children's shelter; serving meals at a soup kitchen; and donating food to an animal shelter.

Her mother wrote: "We often donate to charity, and I've tried to instill a sense of social responsibility in my daughter, but Caitlin has humbled even me by voluntarily giving up her own Christmas gifts to instead benefit those with greater needs than our own."

After the story was published, we received a note from an employee of a residential home for intellectually disabled people. He wrote: "Tonight when she (Caitlin) and her family dropped off the gift basket at the house for our eight residents ... well, I was truly touched by a Christmas spirit I haven't had since I was a young boy."

The full story is at www.quizmas.ca/memory_detail. cfm?id=11.

MAKING IT FUN
Books

Canada Up Close: Canadian Money by Elizabeth Macleod. Did you know that Canada once had $4, $6, and $7 bills? And did you know that a special edition Canadian quarter was once rumoured to be a "spy coin"? This easy-to-read book is filled with kid-friendly facts and historical tidbits about Canadian currency and would be a good choice for any Consumer in Training who enjoys trivia.

Alexander, Who Used to Be Rich Last Sunday by Judith Viorst. If your child is already familiar with Alexander (the main character in the wildly popular book, *Alexander and the Terrible, Horrible, No Good, Very Bad Day*), he'll probably be eager to hear more about his adventures. In this humorous story, Alexander receives a dollar from his grandparents. Despite Alexander's hopes of saving up for a walkie-talkie, he ends up losing his dollar through an unfortunate series of bets, impulse buys, fines, and other mishaps. Although the prices in the book are noticeably dated, the lesson is as relevant as ever. This book is a fun way to demonstrate to your children how easily money can burn a hole in your pocket (along with exposing them to a bit of math for good measure).

Rock, Brock, and the Savings Shock by Sheila Blair and Barry Gott. Rock and Brock might be twins, but their spending habits couldn't be more different. Rock fritters away his money week after week while Brock holds on to his earnings and benefits from Grampa's offer to match his savings. This is a fun story that does a great job of illustrating the magic of compound interest in an easy-to-understand way for young children. Of all the books we read together, this one was Deborah's kids' favourite.

Here's what six-year-old Dahlia took away from the story: "Before you buy anything, you have to think ahead. What will I do with this? Will it be useful? Will it break easily? Is it junk? Ask the store: does this actually work? Save your money and take time to make your decisions before spending."

And here's what her nine-year-old brother learned: "Don't spend every cent you have on junk. Saving is important, but it's okay to buy a few things you want once in a while."

Lemonade for Sale (MathSmart 3) by Stuart J. Murphy and Tricia Tusa. This is an enjoyable book about four friends and their parrot Petey who are looking to raise money to fix up their clubhouse. The kids start a lemonade business, divide up the jobs, and track their daily sales using easy-to-follow bar graphs. It's a nice introduction to learning about bar graphs as well as the idea of entrepreneurship. There are instructions at the end of the book about setting up your own lemonade stand and keeping track of sales.

Start a collection

This is the age where many children become collectors. It may be hockey cards, stamps, rocks, seashells, or whatever. If your child is interested in the idea, see if he'd like to collect coins. It can be fun and maybe even profitable. And it doesn't have to cost a lot.

Many families keep spare change in a glass or jar. Give the coins to your child and tell him to go through them and find as many pennies and nickels from different years as he can. Whenever you bring spare change into the house let your youngster go through it to see if he can find new coins for his collection.

If he takes to the idea, move on to dimes and quarters. Show him the difference between Canadian and U.S. coins and have him look for some stray American coins in the change.

The $400,000 Penny

The most valuable Canadian penny ever struck was a 1936 coin that featured a likeness of King George V on the front and a small dot below the year on the back. It became known as the "Dot Cent," and only three are believed to be in existence. The coin never went into circulation because George V died on January 20 of that year, before it could be distributed by The Royal Canadian Mint. The last time the coin sold at auction, in 2010, it went for $402,000.

Some kids become passionate collectors. If your child seems headed in that direction, buy an album that enables him to display his treasures and will teach him more about the hobby. An excellent starter is the *Deluxe Canadian Coin Collecting Album* by Laura Mahaney and Tammi Salzano, which is published by Scholastic Canada.

First wallet/purse

Now that they're learning how to spend money, they'll need a place to carry it. This is a great time for your Consumers in Training to receive their first wallet and/or purse. It will make them feel oh-so "grown up" as well as raising their excitement level about the idea of money.

Board games

Kids always enjoy playing games with their parents and grandparents. Why not take advantage of that by introducing games that will help them learn about money while they're having fun? That old classic, Monopoly, is perfect for this age group. The original version, which uses paper money, is a good starter because it reinforces the lessons about counting and making change that you've already taught. The newer version uses debit cards and an electronic banking unit, which speeds up the pace of play but eliminates the cash skills.

Monopoly can be a valuable tool in helping to teach kids the basics of finance and investing. But it has to be played as a board game, where you're all sitting around a table together. Electronic versions won't work—the kids are isolated and there is no opportunity for parental interaction.

During the time we were writing this book, we played several games with Deborah's children. During one of them, Jonah became excited at one point by the fact that he had more cash than any of the other players. We paused for a few minutes while his mother explained that was because he had not invested in any houses for his properties. We reinforced that lesson as the game progressed: you have to take some risks if you hope to succeed.

In the end, Dahlia, who was six at the time and playing on the same team as her mom, emerged as the winner. Together, they had gained control of all the cheap properties on the strip between Go and Jail, carefully invested their money in houses and hotels, and then waited until the other players landed on them and were dinged with huge rents.

There are several money and life lessons that can be taught through Monopoly (although don't turn every game into a series of lectures—the idea is to have fun). Here are some:

- Sitting on cash does not win the game.
- You need to take some risks to make big profits.
- Risks need to be carefully thought out.
- If you overextend yourself by taking on too much debt through mortgages or spending too much cash, you will be vulnerable if you are suddenly faced with a big bill.
- Trades need to benefit both sides or they are unlikely to be completed. There has to be a perceived win–win situation. But try to get a small edge and know what that is before you make a trade.
- The game is a combination of skill and luck. You can play well and still lose because the dice don't roll your way. Don't let your kids be discouraged by that. As we said earlier in this chapter, life isn't always fair.

Not everyone is a fan of Monopoly and some people maintain that it teaches the wrong lessons. The main criticism is that it's a cutthroat, winner-take-all game and that losers may leave the table angry and resentful. Our experience is that bad losers are bad losers, whether they are playing Monopoly or checkers. It's the responsibility of parents to help their kids get over that.

In the end, you have to decide if Monopoly is a good game for your kids. But remember that if they don't play it at home, they almost certainly will somewhere else.

If your kids enjoy Monopoly, there are quite a few versions of the game available to download for free to an iPad … a convenient way for them to take the game with them when they're on the go.

Grocery store math

You don't need dice and a board to play money games with kids. Next time you take them to the grocery store, try out some of these fun challenges:

- If you have coupons, have your child help you locate the coupon items, then see if he can use his math skills to calculate the savings.
- Teach him how to comparison shop. For instance, if you're buying toilet paper, show him how to consider both the price and quantity and see if he can tell you which brand is offering the best price. "We could get ten rolls for $1.99 or we could get forty rolls for $4.99. What do you think is the better deal?"
- When you're ready to check out, have him look over the cart and ask him to estimate the total cost of the grocery bill. Of course, he won't get it right but he'll get excited if he comes close, and it

will give him a working sense of your family's food budget.

- If you're paying in cash, have him help you count the money out. When the change comes back, ask him to help you count it to see if it's correct.

Design your own currency

Rainy Saturday with nothing to do? How about a money arts-and-crafts project? Start by Googling images of world currency and showing your child how coins and bills from around the globe all carry images of national leaders and symbols. Then, cutting out bill-sized pieces of paper, ask him to design his own bills for an imaginary country of his own (remember to fill in both the front and the back). When the project is all done, see if he'd like to "buy" a snack from the "restaurant" (your kitchen) with his own currency.

Websites

Are you wondering whether websites and on-line games can really be useful learning tools for financial literacy? We think so. And Caroline Munshaw of Cent$ible Students agrees: "Technology can be an effective tool if the child is comfortable and capable using it. However, it may still require some parental guidance and explanation. It can be a good way to generate conversation."

Ms. Munshaw recommends ING's website Lil' Money Savers as a good place to start. It's at www.lilsavers.ca.

In Lil' Savers MoneyLand, your child will meet a cute cartoon beaver, caribou, polar bear, and loon (do these animals sound familiar?) to take him through the steps of saving, sharing, spending, and growing his money. He can practise his adding skills by counting coins, can play store, and can learn how to keep customers happy by stocking the shelves with the right products. There's also a list of charities to encourage sharing, as well as an allowance app.

On-line games

Although it is not quite as cute as the ING site, Visa Canada has a website filled with useful financial tips and suggestions for Canadian families at http://practicalmoney skills.ca.

One of the games on the site is Ed's Bank, which puts your children to work grabbing fast-moving coins and dropping them into a piggy bank. After a minute of saving, the game then gives you the option of going to the store to spend the money or going back to the piggy bank to save more. Note: unfortunately, there's no way to "win" at this game … except having your child come away with the lesson that spending money is much easier than saving it (and that the satisfaction of buying something is all too fleeting).

If you have older kids in your family, there are games here for them to check out as well, such as Financial Soccer and The Smart Money Quiz. We'll have a review of Financial Soccer in a later chapter.

SUMMING UP

The money lessons are becoming more complex but if your child has a good grounding and you proceed step-by-step things shouldn't be too difficult. These are important years because, for the first time, you are giving your child real responsibilities. He'll have his own allowance, to spend as he wants. He'll be given jobs to do around the house. He'll start to understand the difference between "need" and "want." He'll be asked to decide if he wishes to share his money with those less fortunate and, if so, how much.

It may seem like a lot for kids this age to handle. But with your help, they'll be up to the challenge.

4
SMART SPENDERS—
AGES 9–11

. . . .

I already know all about money.
I've been saving it my whole life.
—JONAH, AGE NINE

GETTING READY

Congratulations, you have a tween in your home. As the nickname suggests, this is a stage of transitions—moving from the tranquil, contented period of late childhood into the turbulent teenage years. And although you might get the occasional eye-roll here and there, thankfully puberty hasn't hit too hard at this stage. (Hold on to your hats, though, because it's just around the corner).

For the most part, tweens are a happy, playful, and industrious bunch. These years are marked by a stronger-than-ever emphasis on peer relationships, the growing desire to belong to a group, and increasing readiness for independence. Socially, your tweens are developing a new understanding of the world around them and their place in it, and they are beginning to grapple with bigger decisions. At school, they are now being given more responsibility to help prepare them for the next stage of learning. At home, financial learning should follow suit.

Most parents who've been putting off teaching their kids lessons about money begin scrambling around this point. Why? Peer pressure starts hitting at this stage and, along with it, a growing desire to be part of the crowd—the tween equivalent of "keeping up with the Joneses." So at this age, your tween is getting ready to move on from Barbies and Lego and is beginning to think about bigger purchases.

. . . .

Tweens

"Tween" is a relatively new term used to describe the age group caught between the duelling desires and demands of childhood and teendom. Here is Deborah's recollection of that time:

When I was eleven years old, I remember being young enough to still want to play with a Cabbage Patch Doll but old enough to want to dress trendily and look stylish. I recall just how important it was to own the "right" things. Back then, those were a pair of Dolphin shorts, a LaCoste T-shirt, a Roots purse, or a Cotton Ginny sweatshirt. With my limited allowance, I couldn't afford them all so I had to make decisions.

Due to the increased marketing push to win the tween dollar, the pressure to own the "right" thing (as well as the prices of these items) has increased over time. As a result, the current generation of kids is feeling the accompanying anxieties at a younger age than ever.

. . . .

Don't be shocked if your tween comes home from school asking for Uggs, iPods, and smartphones. And don't be surprised when she wants you to pay for them. What will your answer be when this happens? You should be prepared ... and so should she. A good understanding of money is suddenly more important than ever. Ideally, you want your tweens to develop a sense of responsibility along with their burgeoning independence. Teaching them how to be smart spenders now will set the foundation for a lifetime of fiscal responsibility.

HOW-TO
Good vs. bad spending

Spending, of course, is the reason money was invented. Spending essentially means taking something we have earned or been given and exchanging it for something we need or want. Way back in the dark ages, this would have meant bartering one type of good for another. Nowadays, we use money. It sounds simple enough, doesn't it? Then why do we make so many mistakes doing it?

Spending is inevitable in our society. And easy. Anybody with a wad of cash burning a hole in his or her pocket can do it. But learning how to spend *wisely* is a skill. Hopefully by this stage, your tween understands the difference between "want" and "need." (If not, it's definitely past time to have that conversation with her.) But does she know the difference between "good" spending and "bad" spending? Probably not. Let's face it, many adults haven't wrapped their heads around this one either. We all know people who have gotten in over their heads by making bad financial decisions. Many others are in the same boat and just not talking about it.

So how can you teach your child the difference between good spending and bad spending? It's actually not that hard. Good spending, basically, means putting time and thought into your purchase to make sure you can afford it. Bad spending is almost always impulsive and ill-considered. As we've mentioned before, this is the time for your child to make mistakes with her money—it's an essential part of the learning process. But handing over an allowance without any advice on how to spend it isn't going to help either. A bit of guidance to help your tween along the way is part of your job.

Here's a checklist of questions your Smart Spender should learn to ask herself before pulling out her wallet:

Is the retailer asking a fair price for this item? Take a moment to think about the amount of allowance this purchase represents. Or the amount of extra time shovelling snow or raking leaves. Is it really worth it?

Have I compared prices and found the best one? With the barrage of flyers littering our doorsteps and the number of stores listing their prices on-line, comparison shopping is easier than ever before.

Am I buying this in the "heat of the moment" or have I given the purchase due consideration? If there's something you really want but you aren't sure you want to spend the money, try walking away for a day or two. If you forget about the item, you didn't need it as much as you thought you did. Money saved!

Can I afford it? Do you have enough money to purchase the item in full? Or will you be asking your parents to give you an advance on your allowance? (This is something we don't recommend, by the way.) Will you have any money left over for other wants or needs?

Can I return it if there's a problem or if I change my mind? If a case of "buyer's remorse" sets in, will you be able to get your money back? Some stores are more lenient than others about their policies. Often, however, once you've handed over your money, you're not going to get it back. (A gift certificate for a return may sound all right but remember: you aren't getting your money back. Your funds are still irrevocably tied to that store). It's important to know what your "out" clause is before you buy.

Do I have a birthday coming up? If so, would it make sense to save your money and ask for the item as a gift instead?

Am I buying this item because I really love it, or is it a trend I'm following to be part of a group? Do I think my friends will like me more if I own this? Has a commercial made me feel like my life will be better if I make this purchase? If the answer is yes to any of these questions, it doesn't necessarily mean your tween shouldn't go ahead with her purchase. Feeling the urge to fit in is a big part of growing up. However, it will do her a world of good to understand the reasons why she's so drawn to these items and maybe even help her feel comfortable making some different choices.

Showing your Smart Spender how to put time and consideration into her purchases is a vital part of teaching her good fiscal responsibility.

Tricks up the sleeves

Unfortunately, stores often use a lot of tricks to lure consumers away from good spending habits. Trumped-up "discounts," fancy ad campaigns, strategically placed "endcaps," and never-ending rotation of new designs and styles are just a few of the multitude of techniques that retailers use to try to mess with your mind and convince you to part with your money.

. . . .

Tween spending power

The Canadian Office of Consumer Affairs website (www. ic.gc.ca/eic/site/oca-bc.nsf/eng/ca02099.html)   reports that, according to YTV's *Tween Report*, Canada's 2.5 million tweens spent some $1.7 billion of their own discretionary income (YTV 2002). But they also increasingly influence family purchases (up to roughly $20 billion), some of which are delegated to them partly because of changing households (such as dual-income parents who are time-stressed).

. . . .

These days, kids are their biggest target, mainly because they have more disposable income than any other demographic. Retailers are all too aware of this and are working overtime to tempt them away from their money. Tweens represent a golden "double-dip" for retailers for the simple reason that they're just as tempted by toys and other childhood trappings as they are by cellphones, lip gloss, and nail polish.

Advertising campaigns attack from every angle, from magazines to TV commercials to websites to billboards to product placement in movies, all of them vying for precious dollars and brand loyalty. A 2012 study by Westcoast Youth Expo found that teens between the ages of twelve and seventeen have an average of $500 per month of disposable income. Your tween is right on the cusp of this age group so it's vital she has the right skills to navigate the coming years.

The first step is to teach your child some "media savvy." As soon as she's watching commercial TV, it's time to explain to her about advertising. Deborah started these lessons when her kids were quite young—about the time they graduated from watching the commercial-free Treehouse channel. The very first time her son, Jonah, told her, "But Mummy, the commercial said … ," he was about six years old.

Here's now she responded:

I took a hard-line approach and gently but firmly explained to him that commercials are the way big businesses try to "trick us out of our money." We had a whole conversation about how advertising is a billion-dollar business and how the commercials try to make you want to buy something you probably don't need and definitely didn't know you wanted until they told you. I explained how there's an invisible war going on in the business world with huge companies fighting over who's going to get our money.

The American PBS network has a great website geared to helping kids get media savvy and learn how to see through the marketing ploys of advertisements. You will find it at http://pbskids.org/dontbuyit.

With games like "The Cost of Cool" and "Take the TV vs. Life Quiz" and challenges called "Design Your Own Cereal Box" and "Be the Ad Detective," this is a great place for your tween to have fun while learning how to assess and question the whirlwind of advertising that constantly bombards us.

The U.S. Federal Trade Commission has also created an on-line game that's designed to help kids understand the difference between a commercial that's telling them something and one that's trying to sell them something. It can be found at Admongo.gov (we were not able to review it as it was undergoing maintenance at the time of writing).

Jonah is almost ten years old as this is being written and right in the thick of tweendom. He still sees things advertised that he wants to have. But he's much more suspicious of the campaigns and messages behind the ads.

· ·

Jonah and the polar bear

Deborah writes: Recently, there was a cute commercial that featured a polar bear hugging a hybrid car user. It aired during the Super Bowl broadcast, which we were watching as a family. When the commercial finished, everyone in the room was won over by the warm-fuzzy feeling we got from the ad. Collectively, we all smiled and said "awwww." Everyone, that is, except nine-year-old Jonah. Concerned that the message of the ad might have been over his head, I turned to him and, in an effort to include him in the moment, asked, "Did you understand the point of that commercial?" And Jonah, very wisely nodded and said, "Yes, Mummy. The company just wants our money. And they're using a cute polar bear to do it."

It's amazing when your children become smarter than you.

· ·

Teaching children to be "commercial savvy" is an important step on the path to financial literacy. Remember, they are still watching you for cues so it's important to practise what you preach. If possible, pre-record your shows so you can fast-forward through the ads altogether. If you can't do that, talk about commercials when they come on and see if your Smart Spender can spot the tricks the advertisers are using to try to win their money. And the next time your family is considering a big purchase, involve your tween in your smart-spending decision. Let her go over the numbers with you, talk about want vs. need, and help her comparison shop for the best price. She'll be much better prepared when the time comes for her to be making these decisions in her own life.

TIME FOR A BANK ACCOUNT

If your tween doesn't have a bank account already, it's time to institutionalize the piggy bank and introduce her to the real world. She already understands the concept of saving—she's been dropping some coins into that piggy every week. Perhaps she's been wondering why her parents don't have their own piggy bank on their dresser. You need to show her how *you* do it.

Her first trip to a bank probably won't excite her much. After all, there's not much to see, no shelves full of money on display, just some harried-looking people standing at the teller stations, some staff working behind them, and a lot of closed office doors. It's up to you to make the visit interesting.

Start by explaining what the bank does. Tell her that it keeps people's money safe for them and in return pays them a small amount for depositing their cash—that's called *interest*, and the fact she's getting money for "free" should interest her.

Tell her that the bank made it possible for Mommy and Daddy to buy the home you all live in (and hope to own at some point). Explain that when you don't have enough money to pay for the house the bank lends you the rest as a mortgage, which you pay back each month. Tell her the bank also helps people to buy cars, start businesses, and do other things.

If you have a safety deposit box, take her into the vault on your first visit. She might find it interesting that people keep so many valuable things in the locked boxes that line the walls. Take out your box and, assuming it's not filled with laundered cash, show her what's in it.

"Here's the deed to our house—it's the proof that we own it."

"Here's Mommy and Daddy's certificate of marriage."

"Here is your birth certificate."

"Here is a solid gold centennial coin that my parents gave me when I was young."

"Here are some Canada Savings Bonds we bought for you the year you were born."

She'll be fascinated.

Once she has a clear idea of what a bank does, it's time to open that first account. You can do that in person while you're there—if the branch manager is available, introduce your tween to her so your child will be able to attach a (hopefully) friendly face to her money.

Most banks also allow you to apply for a children's account on-line, although you have to take your youngster to the bank with appropriate identification for both you and her (a SIN card and birth certificate will do) in order to activate the account.

Almost all banks and many credit unions welcome young people but some are more accommodating than others. For example, while they all offer accounts for those under nineteen, only a few have special programs for your tween.

Bank of Montreal (BMO) is one of them. It offers chequing and savings accounts especially tailored for children under twelve. If your tween lives in Canada and has a social insurance number, she qualifies. (If she doesn't have a social insurance number, what the heck are you waiting for? Apply now!) As long as your child can sign her name, the bank does not require you to co-sign, nor does it have to be a joint account, although that is an option. If she's not yet old enough to sign, the account can be opened by you in trust.

During the spring of 2012, BMO was offering a cash incentive to encourage young people to open accounts. If your youngster deposited twenty-five dollars, the bank would match that, instantly doubling her money. That's a lot of "free" money for a kid—make sure she isn't left with the impression the bank will repeat that every time she makes a deposit. They aren't *that* generous!

BMO's kids' premium rate savings accounts pay a small rate of interest (0.25 percent as of summer 2012), so your youngster won't get rich. But that's more than most of the other major banks offer. A report prepared in August 2012 by Tricia Barry, founder and Executive Director of Money School Canada, a firm that offers in-class financial literacy workshops to elementary, middle and high school students (www.moneycanada.com), found that interest rates on children's savings accounts ranged from a low of 0.01 percent (RBC's Leo's Young Savers Account) to a high of 0.3 percent (CIBC's Advantage for Youth Account).

Of course, you can point out that the piggy bank pays no interest at all—it just swallows the money and lets it sit there. But your youngster may not be impressed with the fact that, in the case of the RBC account, she only receives one cent a year for every hundred dollars she puts in.

Chequing accounts pay no interest but give the kids an opportunity to learn how to use their money to buy things. In the case of BMO, they receive one free set of cheques (after that, they have to pay for them). Just be sure your tween understands that, every time she writes a cheque, the money will disappear from her account and that, once it is all gone, the bank will return the cheques and charge a penalty. If you aren't sure she's ready for chequing just yet, start with a simple savings account and work up to the idea of cheques later.

BMO also provides a debit card for children's accounts, but give it some careful thought before agreeing to it. Debit cards make it very easy—perhaps *too* easy—for youngsters to spend their money and may have the effect of getting them hooked on plastic at an early age. Having to lay out real cash for a purchase may encourage your child to think a little harder about whether or not she really wants the item. We'll have more to say about debit cards a little later in this chapter.

BMO also offers special accounts with more sophisticated features for teens (age thirteen to eighteen) and for students and recent graduates. You can check out the details at www.bmo.com/home/personal/banking/everyday/youth-and-students/kids-accounts.

Most of the other banks have one-size-fits-all accounts for young people under nineteen. Terms and conditions vary but may include no monthly fees, no transaction costs, a debit card, tiered interest, free access to mobile, on-line, and telephone banking, and more.

Here's where you can find additional information:

Royal Bank's Leo's Young Savers Account: www.rbc royalbank.com/products/deposits/leo-young-savers-account.html.

CIBC's Advantage for Youth: www.cibc.com/ca/chequing-savings/advantage-for-youth.html.

TD Canada Trust's Youth Account: www.tdcanada trust.com/products-services/banking/accounts/savings-accounts/youth.jsp.

Scotiabank's Student Accounts: www.scotiabank.com/ca/en/0,,14,00.html.

HSBC Premier Family Services: www.hsbc.ca/1/2/en/personal/hsbcpremier/family.

Canadian Western Bank Youth Account: www.cwbank.com/personal_banking/personal_accounts.htm.

If you deal with a credit union, check their website or make inquiries the next time you're in. Some, but not all, have special plans for children. For example, Toronto-based DUCA Credit Union offers a bonus of one dollar for every net increase of fifty dollars in a child's account, to a maximum of twelve dollars per year.

You can find a summary of Tricia Barry's report at www.prlog.org/11964047-let-the-children-pay-are-banks-really-helping-parents-to-teach-the-value-of-savings.html.

A bank account checklist

Here is a list of things to ask about when opening a child's first bank account.

Type of account. Most first accounts are savings, but some have chequing privileges.

Fees. Make sure both you and your tween have a clear understanding of all the fees involved. Usually, savings accounts are free, but writing a cheque may cost money, there may be a limit on the number of free debit card uses, and withdrawals using another bank's ATM will have a service charge. Warns Tricia Barry: "Some banks have extra charges that could slowly erode the youngster's precious savings."

Interest rate. How much will your child's money earn? Some accounts pay almost nothing, so look for the best return available.

Promotions. Are there any sweeteners? Does your child get a bonus for opening an account or making deposits?

Debit card. Is there one included with the account? If so, find out the terms and conditions. For example, some cards allow a limited number of free transactions before a fee is charged.

Other perks. A few children's cards offer adult-style benefits, such as reward points.

On-line access. Find out if your child can access the account on-line and, if so, arrange to have it set up. It will make it much easier to monitor and to explain transactions.

Conditions. A few banks restrict these accounts to children of existing customers.

THE FIRST DEBIT CARD

Like it or not, we're moving ever closer the reality of a cashless society. And, according to a 2012 survey conducted on behalf of PayPal Canada, most Canadians like it. In fact, 71 percent of respondents reported being "comfortable with never having to handle cash to make a purchase." That's a big increase from 2011, which suggests the idea of a cashless society is rapidly gaining momentum. Not only that, 25 percent of the survey respondents said they have already gone more than a week without using cash.

There's no reason to presume this trend won't continue. By the time your child is grown, we might indeed be living in a cashless world—it won't be just the penny that has disappeared, but all tangible money. All financial transactions will take place electronically.

A generation ago, that would have seemed like the stuff of science fiction. Now it could be a reality by the time your child reaches middle age.

Some history

Debit cards are simply a convenient way to draw money from a bank account. In the past, the most common ways of doing that were by writing a cheque or making a trip to the bank or ATM to withdraw cash. The introduction of the first debit cards in Canada by Saskatchewan credit unions in 1977 made it possible for people to access their accounts electronically and use the money for retail purchases without the need for cash.

The idea didn't catch on right away, however. It wasn't until the early 1990s that the major banks stuck their collective toes in the water with a series of pilot projects aimed at testing the reliability of the new system and to gauge potential public interest. There wasn't a lot of initial enthusiasm. By then, people were used to the idea of shopping with credit cards, which meant several weeks would elapse before the bills actually had to be paid. With a debit card, the money disappeared from a bank account in an electronic instant. Moreover, some people distrusted the accuracy and security of the system and worried that their accounts might be compromised. After all, if an incorrect charge appeared on a credit card statement, you just didn't pay it. With debit cards, it would be a fight to get back money that was already out the door.

But the banks persisted, and in 1994 the first nationwide debit card payment system was introduced, Interac Direct Payment (IDP). By the end of the 1990s, about 50 percent of retailers had signed on to the system. By 2009, that was up to 99 percent—almost total acceptance. Today, far more transactions are completed using debit cards than cash, and the gap is widening.

Is this the time?

Your child will have to learn how to manage a debit card sooner or later. If the bank account you set up for her offers a free debit card as an option, it's probably a good idea to take advantage of it as long as your tween is able to understand how the card works and what it does.

Keep your explanation simple. Once the bank account has been opened, show your child how much money is in it, either in her bank book (increasingly rare) or on-line. Then show her the debit card and explain that, if she uses it, the cost of her purchase will immediately be taken from her account. Explain that once all the money in the account is gone, the debit card will be rejected until she deposits more money in the account.

Try an experimental run the next time you are shopping with her. If she says she wants to buy something, have her use the debit card. When you get home, check her account on-line and show her how quickly the money vanished and how much she has left.

The advantage of a debit card is that your tween will never go into debt. She can only spend as much money as she has in her account, no more. That makes it much safer than allowing her to have a credit card at this age.

BUDGET BASICS

Budgets are good for you, like healthy eating. The problem is that, like spinach, they're not much fun. Many adults use any possible excuse to avoid the perceived drudgery of creating and monitoring a family budget. Why should the kids be any different?

Perhaps this explains why fewer than half of the more than 3,000 post-secondary students who participated in a 2011 national survey sponsored by the British Columbia Securities Commission had a budget to control their expenses. Either they had never been taught how to manage a budget or they lacked the motivation to follow through.

Some education systems are starting to teach this information at the high school level but we think it needs to start sooner—with you, the parent. The best way to introduce the subject is to take a positive and creative approach to the concept of budgeting. Don't present it as a chore. Instead, suggest to your child that it's a way to get more for the money she receives from allowances, gifts, and odd jobs. Something along the lines of this: "If we do it this way, you'll be able to get the book you want now and have enough for that new game by the end of the month."

It's important not to overwhelm the kids with too much information at the start. Some experts suggest using the family budget as a learning tool, explaining what's in it and how it works. We agree, but only up to a certain point. A family budget can be complex, and the numbers will be far beyond anything your child can grasp at this point. Moreover, many of the expenses will be meaningless to a young person and may get you bogged down in explanations you prefer to avoid at this stage. (Do you really want to discuss the cost of a bottle of wine or why you need to spend money on certain types of prescriptions?)

The better approach is to work with your children to create a simple budget that is tailored to their age and skill level. You'll find a sample worksheet you can copy on the next page.

Name

Month

Income

Allowance

Gifts

Work

Other

Total

Fixed expenses

Bus fare

School lunches

Savings

Other

Total

Optional expenses

Snacks

Movie

Books

Games and toys

Gifts

Other

Total

Total income

Total expenses

Difference

This simple budget operates on your child's level. She starts by writing in her name, which gives her ownership, and the month. Next, she enters the amount of money she expects to receive during the month from her allowance, gifts, chores around the house, the Tooth Fairy, or whatever. You'll have to help her with that at the start, but she'll soon be able to do her own estimates.

Now comes the fun part—spending. Begin by explaining that there are certain costs she is expected to pay from her own money. These will vary depending on the circumstances, but they might include bus fare, school lunches, and, if she has one, part of the cost of a cellphone. (Some families supply kids with cellphones for safety reasons with the caution that any excess charges are the child's responsibility.) Even if there are no fixed expenses, some money should be allocated for savings each month.

Optional expenses come out of whatever amount is left once the fixed costs have been allocated. Here's where you have to work with the child to make good decisions. She might want to go to the movies once a week, but if her budget doesn't allow that, she needs to adjust. You can show her that if she spends too much on candy, she won't have enough left for the new book all her friends have been talking about. In this way, you can teach her how to make better financial decisions and help her understand that the amount of money she has available will only stretch so far. You may also motivate her to earn more, perhaps by taking on some extra chores, setting up a lemonade stand, or holding a mini garage sale for old toys and games.

Vacation budgets

Family vacations are always special times, whether it's a simple camping trip or a grand excursion to Disney World. Because it's a holiday, there is always a tendency to throw caution to the wind and overspend. Adults are sometimes as susceptible to this temptation as the kids, so it may help your own finances if you work out a vacation budget with your child before leaving home.

The holiday budget may look a little different from the regular monthly one. Here's a sample.

Name	
Holiday	
Amount to spend	
Savings	
Allowance	
From Mom and Dad	
Other	
Total	
What I want	
Souvenirs	
Shows	
Snacks	
Other	
Total	
Total income	
Total expenses	
Difference	

The amount available to spend should be clearly set before leaving home. You may offer to contribute some money but make sure your youngster understands that there will be no more once the total amount has been spent. Give her a lot of leeway as to how the money is used—this is a special event, after all. But don't tolerate any "I want this" or "buy me that" antics. If she clearly understands the rules before leaving home, the whole trip will go a lot more smoothly.

MAKING IT FUN
Websites—Debit cards and ATMs

Here's an easy and fun way to demystify debit cards and ATMs. The suggestion comes from Caroline Munshaw, co-founder of Cent$ible Students. She recommends a website created by the Ottawa Community Loan Fund which includes simulated ATMs and debit card terminals that your kids can practise on. They were originally created to help newcomers to Canada learn about our banking system, but they're also great tools for tweens to learn about banking without sharing passwords or confidential information with anyone. To get these on-line "machines" to work, use the password 1234 (easy to remember for these purposes, but obviously not a good password to use in the real world).

The on-line ATM machine can be found at http://oclf. org/atm/ATM.html. The first prompt asks you to insert your card, which you do by clicking on the picture of a bank card on the right of the screen. You'll then be asked for the language of your choice—the site is available in both English and French versions. Next, enter the PIN and click on OK. Once that is done, six choices will appear, just as with a real ATM machine. Go through them with your child.

Withdrawal. When that button is clicked, two options will appear: Chequing and Savings. Have your tween select one. A notice will then appear saying that the operator of the ATM charges a fee of $1.50 for a withdrawal. This is the time to explain that sometimes withdrawals are not free and to remind your child to find out the rules that apply at her bank. If she agrees to the fee, she will be asked to enter the amount she wishes to withdraw. The machine only accepts multiples of twenty dollars. Once she clicks OK, the ATM will dispense the requested amount (not real cash, unfortunately) and ask if she wants a receipt. Have her click OK and an on-line receipt will appear. Explain to her that the receipt will show that twenty dollars (or whatever amount she chose) has been deducted from her account.

Transfer. This option is used to transfer money from one account to another. Explain to your child that if she has both a savings and a chequing account and wants to write a cheque, she may have to move some money from one account to the other.

Bill payment. Your tween isn't likely to have any bills, but since you're on the website anyway, you may wish to explain how an ATM can be used for payments. After this button is clicked and the type of account chosen, three dummy company names and account numbers appear: a cable company, a telephone company, and an insurance company. Choose any one, enter an amount, and the machine will process the payment and issue a receipt.

Deposit. A bank machine doesn't only dispense money and pay bills. It also accepts deposits. Click on this button and show your tween how it works and where the deposit envelope would be inserted on a real ATM.

Fastcash. Some machines offer a choice of withdrawing specific amounts of money, rather than entering a figure. In this case the options are $20, $60, $100, $140, and $200. Have your child select the amount she wants and hit OK. (Don't be surprised if she chooses $200; it's only pretend money after all.)

Account balance. After all the transactions have been completed, your tween will want to know how much money she has left. Click the Account Balance button to find out. She may be pleasantly surprised to see that she has over $1,000. Don't let it go to her head!

For the debit card machine, go to http://oclf.org/atm/debit.html. This one is a lot simpler. It's a reproduction of the kind of terminal your child would be handed if she used a debit card at a shop in the mall. After choosing a language, she'll be asked to swipe her card—click on the icon at the top right to do that. She'll then be asked to approve a purchase amount. The machine may also ask for approval of a "terminal fee" of twenty-five cents—this seems to come up randomly. She may also be asked if she wants to include a tip; you can explain that this is done with restaurant purchases and in a few other places, like a beauty salon. Next, she'll be asked for her PIN (1234).

The machine will then process the transaction and flash an "approved" notice. We never received a "declined" in several tries, but you should explain that's what will happen if the account does not have enough money to cover the purchase. Finally, a receipt summarizing the transaction and any others that have been processed will appear.

There is a lot more useful material on this site including a Newcomer Finances Toolkit that provides basic information on a wide range of financial subjects including banking, credit, insurance, income tax, government support programs, investments, and fraud. If you think you need to learn more about any of these topics, take a look at http://oclf.org/newcomer-finances-toolkit.

Banking games

Country Bank of Massachusetts has some on-line banking games you can try with your kids at www.bankingkids.com/pages/00947/bank_index.html. There are three portals: preschool, elementary, and teens. You can choose the one that is most appropriate. Some of the games are pretty basic and your child may quickly get bored with them but a few may be instructive.

Kid Review: Planet Orange

Address: www.orangekids.ca

Sponsor: ING Direct

Comments: At the beginning of the game, I had to fill out a registration form asking me to create an account. It asked for simple things like a username, password, and my parents' email address.

The plot of the game is that you're an astronaut exploring a planet—Planet Orange. You have two space guides, Amy and Cedric. You can go on missions to earn space badges, visit the Orangeopolis stock exchange, take a quiz, or spend money at the space station arcade.

Planet Orange has four continents, and on each continent there are places you can go. Each place teaches you about a different part of money, such as reasons to save, the history of money, jobs and paycheques, taxes, and more. At the end of each continent tour, you take a quiz that tests you on the information you learned. When you complete the quiz you earn "Obux," which is short for "Orange Bucks"—the local currency.

You can also earn Obux by taking jobs that involve answering questions about math and other school subjects. The job pays you Obux depending on the difficulty. Unfortunately, you can only take one job every twelve real-life hours, which was a little disappointing, but I assume it's so kids will keep coming back to the site daily.

You can use Obux to buy different things for your space station, such as games and furniture. But you also need to save some of your money to buy fuel because every time you travel it burns fuel. If you run out of fuel you can't travel anymore, which means you can't earn money except for your job every twelve hours, so you could get into quite a fix if you spend all your money at once. This is an important feature of the game because it teaches kids that you can spend some money on fun stuff but you need to save some for the necessities.

Strong Points: A lot of games designed to teach kids about money are very basic and cheaply made, so they get tedious and boring very fast. Planet Orange is intricate and exciting. It's a game that I could see kids playing daily and having a lot of fun. The game is really good at teaching kids about a wide range of financial information, from things they can use right away to things they will need when they get older.

Weak Points: I found this game fun and educational, but it's more mature than they suggest. On the website they say it's for kids from grades one to six but I would recommend it for kids from grades three to six, because a large majority of the game is just listening to people tell you facts and it's challenging to navigate until you get the hang of it.

There weren't really any major technical flaws except the load times were a little long.

Favourite Feature: I really liked the idea of Obux. It was a very innovative way of teaching kids about money by giving them a large amount of money to spend, the ability to earn more if they want to work, and the option to save or spend their money. It's a good way to learn by experience, which is the fastest and easiest way to learn.

Summary: With no advertising on the site and a parental notification system in place, this is a fun and safe way to learn about money.

Rating: 4/5 stars

Reviewer: Daylen, age fourteen

Videos

Caine's Arcade

Around the time we were researching this book, a video about a nine-year-old boy from East Los Angeles went viral. Unless you were living under a rock, you probably saw or heard about Caine Monroy, a young man who built an entire cardboard arcade in the front of his dad's used auto parts store. As soon as his cardboard arcade was ready (complete with his own cardboard office, cardboard claw machine, and cardboard ticket feeder), Caine waited patiently for people to come and play his games.

Unfortunately, with most of his dad's business happening on-line, customers were scarce. Caine instinctively did what any good businessman would do ... he bundled his prices and came up with a deal you couldn't pass up (one dollar will get you four turns, but two dollars will get you a Funpass worth 500 turns!).

One fortuitous day, a young filmmaker dropped in to buy a door handle for his car and bought a Funpass. He was so impressed with Caine's passion, determination, and entrepreneurial spirit, he filmed a short movie about the arcade and posted it here: www.cainesarcade.com. In addition, he set up a fund where people could donate to Caine's college fund. And the rest, as they say, is history. At last count, Caine's educational fund had over $200,000 in international donations and there was a steady stream of game-playing customers at his arcade.

The moral of the story is that anybody with passion, imagination, and a big idea can make a go of a business ... regardless of their age. If your tween comes to you with a "zillion-dollar idea," nurture her ambition and offer her support in any way you can. Luck and hard work are important elements of any successful business venture, but so is spirit. There's a famous quote by Les Brown that's worth keeping in mind: "Shoot for the moon ... even if you miss, you'll land among the stars."

Apps

Kid Review: *Save! The Game*—**app for iPhone, iPad**

Comments: *Save! The Game* tries to teach kids to not spend all their money the second they get it on junky stuff like candy bars and video games. It does that by making the "iwannas"—these are the candy bars and video games—steal your money. At the end of each level, it tells you tips about money, like you don't really *need* that candy bar ... you *want* it. The way you get money is you have to run around the levels looking for coins on the ground. The iwannas can get your money by running into you or, if you are in front of money, they can run into the money.

Strong points: There are some good tips such as don't waste your money on junk food and that you should save up your money for more expensive things.

Weak points: Sometimes the main character is hard to manoeuvre around the levels.

Favourite feature: Putting the money in the bank for extra points is my favourite part of the game. It is a challenge because some of the "iwannas" are guarding the bank.

Rating: 3/5

Reviewer: Jonah, age nine

Books

Money, Money, Money. Where It Comes From, How To Spend It, Save It, and Make It by Eve Drobet. Covering everything from the history of money to making money to banking, saving, credit, and interest, this Canadian book explains it all in a kid-friendly format. It's filled with colourful illustrations and fun facts. For instance, did you know the 1954 one-dollar bill was taken out of circulation because Canadians thought they saw the face of the devil in the curls of Queen Elizabeth's hair? Kids will find lots of useful information in this book. There are even sections about protecting yourself from identity theft and on-line fraud … advice many adults could benefit from reading as well.

The Secret Life of Money: A Kid's Guide to Cash by Kira Vermond and Clayton Hanmer. This Canadian-authored book demystifies the "secret life of money" and breaks it down in a way kids can easily understand and, more importantly, enjoy. Addressing kids directly, the book talks about the importance of learning about debt, saving, and spending before they become adults "who may already be in serious debt because no one taught them how to handle their money in the first place." Smart stuff! Full of helpful information and written in an easy, accessible voice, this is a book that belongs on every Smart Spender's shelf.

The Lemonade War by Jacqueline Davies.

The Toothpaste Millionaire by Jean Merrill. Both of these books got "two thumbs up" from our tween reviewers. Both are fun, light novels about entrepreneurial-minded kids who start businesses. With cleverly imbedded lessons on finances, marketing, and product pricing, these are the kinds of books that are rife with information … but written so well that kids don't even realize they're learning. First published in 1972, *The Toothpaste Millionaire* has become a modern-day classic. *The Lemonade War* is followed up by two sequels, *The Lemonade Crime* and *The Bell Bandit*, for young readers left wanting more.

Games

The Settlers of Catan: This is a terrific game! It doesn't involve money per se, but it teaches youngsters about the productive use of land and resources and how to utilize the wealth generated by them to build roads and communities.

The game was created by a German, Klaus Teuber, whose formal education, believe it or not, was as a dental technician (he holds a master's degree in the profession). In the 1980s, he decided he would rather spend his time designing board games than probing around in people's mouths and came up with the idea for *Barbarossa*, which won Germany's prestigious Spiel des Jahres (Game of the

Year) award in 1988. He followed that with *The Settlers of Catan* in 1995, which also won a Spiel des Jahres and was named U.S. Board Game of the Year in 1996. It went on to become a huge international hit. It is now available in more than thirty languages and has sold more than fifteen million units worldwide. Despite this success, however, many people are not familiar with it. Take our advice and buy it—this game is an excellent introduction to the concept of wealth creation.

The basic game is played with three or four participants (there is an expansion available that adds up to two more players). The setting is the remote island of Catan. What makes this different from other board games is that the island can take on a different configuration each time. The game comes with thirty-seven hexagonal region tiles (called hexes) which can be set up in any way the players desire within a sea border. Each tile represents a different type of terrain and produces its own resource:

Forest = wood (lumber)
Hills = clay (bricks)
Pasture = sheep (wool)
Fields = grain (wheat)
Mountains = rocks (ore)

There is also a desert hex, which produces nothing of value and where a robber hides out who steals resources from players when given the opportunity.

The goal is to accumulate resources and use them to build settlements, roads, and eventually cities. Each settlement or city enables a player to earn more resources. Players win points for the longest road. Resources can also be used to buy development cards. These award points for building churches, markets, libraries, an army, and more.

There is a lot of action in this game. Players can trade resource cards to attempt to gain an edge over their opponents, but there is a danger in hoarding them because the robber preys on those who own too many cards. Trading can also be done on a favourable basis by gaining control of seaports.

The first player to accumulate ten Victory Points is declared the winner. Playing time is about ninety minutes.

The manufacturer's suggested age range for this game is ten and up, but those polled by the boardgamegeek.com website suggested eight and up is more appropriate. Even younger kids may enjoy it; six-year-old Dahlia grasped the concept quickly and almost won the first time she played.

If the basic game is too complex, there is a simpler version called *Catan: Junior,* which the makers say is suitable for children five and older. It takes place on a group of islands, each of which generates a specific resource: wood, goats, molasses, swords, and gold. Players build ships and hideouts and try to stay clear of the Spooky Ghost Captain.

The success of the original game spawned several expansions and spin-offs including *The Rivals of Catan*, *The Struggle for Catan*, and even *Catan in Space*. There are also Catan history games: *Settlers of America*, *Settlers of the Stone Age*, and *Struggle for Rome*. In each case, the setting changes, but in most cases the principle is the same: use talent and resources to build a new society. However, some games are much more warlike than others (e.g., *Struggle for Rome*). If that's a problem for you, stick with the original version.

Settlers and some of the other games are also available in electronic versions for PCs, Xbox, iPhone, iPad, Android, Nintendo DS, and Amazon Kindle. However, we think they are much more fun in the social context of a board game.

There are demos of all the games at the official Catan website, www.catan.com. There's also a newsletter, a Facebook page, tournaments, and much more if your kids fall in love with the game.

SUMMING UP

You've taken your child to a whole new level. She now has a bank account, her own cheques, and perhaps a debit card. You've helped her understand such sophisticated concepts as advertising and marketing. She's learned how to become a savvy shopper by asking key questions before she makes a purchase decision. And all this before she becomes a teenager. Did you know as much at that age?

5
EARNING APPRENTICES—
AGES 12–13

* * * * * * * * * * * * *

Dad, can I have $300 for a video game?
—KEYNEN, AGE THIRTEEN

GETTING READY

Contradictions abound as your child continues to morph into a teen before your very eyes. Legally, he's old enough to stay home alone and even care for younger children. But emotionally he's still not mature enough to be fully independent. Physically, he looks more and more like an adult with every passing week. But in the grand scheme of life, he's still a puppy. Yup, it's a confusing time for everyone. And let's not forget all the huge emotional, physical, and social changes he's facing.

Most likely, you've already noticed how your child's friends have begun to take precedence over his family. He increasingly craves independence and will be starting to seek out ways to separate himself from you emotionally (cue the onslaught of eye-rolling and bored-sounding one-word answers). You might start to find that giving him advice is proving difficult as he "knows it all already." But don't let that stop you from trying to teach him how to deal with the new responsibilities that come along with his growing independence … increasing financial responsibilities being among them.

HOW-TO
Ready for more

Parents, this is the age where you'll want to start increasing your kid's allowance and, along with it, the number of things he'll be expected to pay for himself. Don't think of it as a greater expense to you. Instead, consider it as a transfer of responsibilities. In other words, spending shouldn't be just about candy and comic books anymore. You'll have to decide what works best for your family, but by this age many kids can be expected to help shell out for some of their own expenses like lunches, movie tickets, clothing, bus fares, and school supplies.

Do you think this is too early for him to be footing even just a few of his own bills? Think again. The earlier he starts understanding how to stretch his dollars, the better prepared he'll be when the financial burdens of "real life" hit in a few years. Remember, you can always start the list with a few small expenses and increase the amount over time.

Hopefully, your Earning Apprentice understands the concept of budgeting (as discussed in Chapter 4) by now. If not, it's time for another review. The more he understands how to prioritize his spending money, the better he'll be at handling his new financial responsibilities. For instance, if you've decided to provide him with a cellphone, make sure he has a good understanding of how the billing works before you send him off with this new prize. Better yet, why not give him the job of researching and comparing different wireless plans?

- -

Teens and cells

Whether or not you like the idea, your teen will probably get a cellphone at some point and you'll be on the hook for at least part of the cost. According to a 2009 survey by Solutions Research Group Canada, 71 percent of Canadians kids age twelve to nineteen own a cellphone.

- -

Once you've decided on a plan together, review the monthly phone and data limits and explain to him how he'll be responsible for any charges over and above the base monthly fee you've agreed to pay. And be sure to have this discussion *before* you give him the phone so there'll be no surprises down the road. After all, how many horror stories have you heard about teenagers unknowingly running up their cellphone bill because nobody was holding them accountable for the charges? Or worse, because nobody explained how the charges worked?

Earning outside the home: extra pocket money

It's expensive being a teenager these days. With ever-growing social pressures and shifting priorities, it's no wonder so many kids start to look for alternative sources of income as they approach their teen years. To finance his growing wants, your child might start looking for extra earning opportunities outside the home. But is this the right age to start? Caroline Munshaw of Cent$ible Students says yes, "as long as your child has the desire and the motivation. If they have that, there is usually something you can find that is age appropriate for them to begin learning and earning."

. . . .

Kid quote

If I won $1,000 in a lottery, I'd buy clothes.—Sarah, age fourteen

. . . .

Since you have to be eighteen years old to buy a lottery ticket legally in Canada, a job is the best way to go if your child wants more money for things like clothes or electronics. Babysitting, accompanying a younger child home from school, shovelling a neighbour's driveway, dog walking, feeding a neighbour's pet while they're out of town ... maybe even organizing a neighbourhood garage sale ... of course these are just a few examples, but there are endless ways your Earning Apprentice can supplement his income.

Ms. Munshaw recommends choosing a job that works within the parameters of your family's belief system and comfort level. She also suggests having "some discussion around the task, to make sure your child understands their responsibilities, including their personal safety."

Looking for a job opportunity that can incorporate some of your child's strengths and interests is a good place to start. Is he particularly advanced at tennis? Piano? Reading? Then perhaps he could tutor a struggling student or, if he is advanced enough, a gifted one. Or maybe he has a fascination with cars? How about a neighbour-hood car-washing business? Encouraging your Earning Apprentice to come up with a job that he'll enjoy doing (as well as one that's within his range of abilities) will greatly improve his chance of success. A concept Gordon always raised his children with was this: "Do what you love and the money will come."

. . . .

Doing what you love

Billy, a fourteen-year-old member of our extended family, has a passion for baseball. He not only plays the game but has read the rule book from cover to cover.

Last summer he got a job umpiring Little League games at a nearby park. It paid twenty dollars per game, and he got an average of four games a week.

He saved the money to buy a cellphone. At a rate of eighty dollars a week plus some extra money earned mowing lawns, it didn't take him very long.

. . . .

Before he gets started, be sure to discuss your child's earning expectations with him. Is there something specific he's saving up for? How much extra money is he hoping to earn at this new job? What kind of time frame is he giving himself to earn it? Without throwing cold water on his ambitions, help him project a realistic schedule of his potential earnings. It's not unusual for kids of this age to get caught up in grandiose "get-rich-quick" dreams. Helping him set reasonable goals for himself will save disappointment in the long run.

Deborah: In a jam

Back in the 1980s when I was a tween, my best friend Joanne and I decided we would sell containers of homemade berry jam to earn extra spending money. Excited at the idea of all the cash we'd be making, my friend and I spent hours trekking through the thickets that grew in our local ravine, picking raspberries and blackberries until our arms and legs were thoroughly bloodied and scratched. After crushing the berries and sweetening the resulting mush with sugar, we set up our "jam stand" and waited for customers. Sad to say, we didn't have many. Looking back, I think we might have had a respectable amount of sales if we'd bothered to consult a recipe book ... something a quick Google search would take care of nowadays.

Note to former tween self: jam needs to be cooked!

Remember, to truly appreciate the value of money (as well as appreciating his hard-working parents), at some point your child must participate in earning an income of his own. Earning some of his own money is invaluable training—even at this young age, he'll learn real lessons about punctuality, responsibility, leadership, and respect, as well as the importance of a strong work ethic. This is the kind of training that will pave the way for that all-important "first real job" in the coming years. Ideally, when the time comes for him to fill out that first resumé, he'll have some experience under his belt along with perhaps even a reference or two.

THE ABCs OF INVESTING

Now that your Earning Apprentice is making some money and has learned how to spend it and save it, the next lesson is investing. Think he's too young? Nonsense! It's never too early to learn about investing. Warren Buffett was only eleven when he bought his first stock. If you don't believe your budding teen is ready for such complexities, check out the YouTube video of young Victoria Grant railing against the Canadian banking system. It's an eye-opener, whether or not you agree with her opinions.

By this time, you should have introduced the most basic form of investing to your kids by explaining to them how their bank accounts earn interest (not much, it's true, but it's a start). Now it's time to go to the next level and teach them about compounding—how to use other people's money to make even more money.

Begin by explaining the Rule of 72. It's a fundamental investing concept that is easy to understand and powerful in its implications. Here's how it works. Simply divide 72 by the annual return on an investment. The result is the number of years it will take for the original amount of money to double.

For example, if your child has $100 in a bank account that is earning interest at a rate of 1 percent, it will take seventy-two years before that money grows to $200. Your kid is not going to be impressed with that—he probably can't think beyond next year, much less seventy-two years into the future.

But now you tell him that if he finds a way to earn 4 percent on his money, he'll double it in eighteen years. That seems a little more reasonable. And if he can earn 6 percent, his original $100 will grow to $200 in just twelve years. This simple math exercise will quickly help him understand why it makes sense to look for a better place to keep his savings than in a bank account.

However, there's another side to the equation that your young teen needs to understand before you set him free in the investment world. That's the element of risk. It's an investment truism that the greater the potential return, the more risk there is of loss. After grasping the implication of the Rule of 72, your child may want to find somewhere that his savings can earn 10 percent, thereby doubling in 7.2 years. Guess what? Everyone else would like the same thing. The problem is that in this period of low interest rates and volatile stock markets, securities that offer 10 percent return potential are hard to find and fraught with risk.

The worst thing that can happen to a budding investor is to lose money right out of the gate. These kids don't have a lot of savings, and they tend to put a disproportionate value on what they have. Losing a chunk of that money because they become greedy and take too much risk can be devastating. Gordon once had a golfing buddy who adamantly refused to have anything to do with the stock market because he had taken a big hit early in life. He never got over the psychological trauma.

So encourage your fledgling investor to be careful at the beginning. Look for ways to improve on the interest rate being paid on the bank account without putting the money at serious risk.

Canada Premium Bonds and their provincial equivalents are one place to start. They're as safe as bank accounts (which are protected by deposit insurance), and they generally offer a slightly better return. But that advantage won't be impressive—perhaps only a quarter or half a percentage point better than a high interest account. CPBs can be cashed anytime but interest is only paid to the last anniversary date.

Our preference for a first investment would be a conservative mutual fund with a solid track record. A few financial institutions, TD Bank among them, allow the purchase of their no-load mutual funds for a minimum of just $100. Most kids this age could pull together that much cash if they wanted to. Begin with a balanced fund that invests more or less equally in bonds and stocks. The average annual return of a fund of this type (known as Canadian neutral balanced, in technical terms) was 5.7 percent over the three years to the end of May 2012. At that rate, an investment would double in 12.6 years.

There are three advantages to a no-load mutual fund. First, it costs nothing to get in. None of your child's money will be spent on sales commissions. Second, it provides instant diversification. The money is invested in a portfolio of stocks and bonds, selected by professional money managers. Third, it's easy to monitor. There is only one security to watch, and its performance is updated every month on the company website.

As the years pass, your child can put some money in other mutual funds or may even decide to try the stock market. But that's a giant step away. At this point, the main objective is to help him to understand what investing is all about and get him started in a low risk way.

· ·

The difference between stocks and bonds

This is as good a time as any to teach your child the difference between the two most basic types of investments: stocks and bonds.

Very simply, bonds involve lending money and receiving interest for it. Stocks represent a share of ownership in a business.

Here's one way to explain it. Suppose Bill, who lives next door, tells your son he wants to start mowing lawns in the neighbourhood to earn some extra money. However, he needs some cash to buy and operate a power lawn mower. Bill knows your son has some savings. Can he borrow some? He'll pay it back with interest.

Your son has three choices. He can agree to lend Bill the money and take an IOU promising repayment within two months at, say, 3 percent interest. In effect, he is investing in a short-term bond.

The second option is to tell Bill that instead of lending him the money he'd like to buy an interest in the lawn mowing business. In exchange for putting up the cash for the mower, your son asks for 15 percent of the money Bill earns. What he is really doing is purchasing stock in Bill's company and asking for a dividend in return.

The third option is to refuse the request. If Bill has the reputation of talking big and doing little, that might be the best idea (too much risk). But if Bill is a serious, dependable kid, then investing in his lawn mowing business, either through a loan or a share, may be a smart move.

. . . .

TAKING OFF THE TRAINING WHEELS

Here's a common dilemma: Once your child's disposable income is on the rise, should you interfere if you don't agree with his choices? Or is it best to let him learn from his mistakes? What if you know he's making a bad decision … one he'll eventually regret?

Say, for example, your thirteen-year-old son has been diligently saving his money for a laptop of his own. He's been doing extra jobs around the house and shovelling driveways up and down the street all winter, and you're bursting with pride at his determination and perseverance. Then one day a flyer is delivered to your mailbox advertising a liquidation sale at the local electronics store. Sucked in by the sale, your pride and joy gleefully announces his plans to drop a chunk of his savings on the latest version of *Mario Kart*. Do you step in with your wagging finger and pearls of wisdom, barring his way as he tries to run out the door? Or do you stand aside and let him blow his hard-earned money?

Of course, there's nothing wrong with offering your child some gentle words of guidance. As a concerned and involved parent, it's part of the job description. But please believe us when we tell you that controlling his spending is not going to do him any good. If he's determined to make bad financial choices with his own money, you must let him. Remember, mistakes are an integral part of any learning process.

Think back a few years to when he was learning to ride a two-wheeler. Once those training wheels came off, you offered him words of encouragement while you helped guide his bike down the sidewalk, keeping a firm grip on the handlebars so he wouldn't lose his balance and fall off. But, eventually, the time came when you had to let go and let him try riding it all by himself. And, of course, he fell. And maybe he skinned his knee or scraped his elbow. But he got back on and tried again and eventually learned to ride by himself. If you hadn't ever let go of that bike, he'd never have learned how to do it.

Now it's time to apply those same principles to money. Tricia Barry, Executive Director of Money School Canada, agrees:

> Parental interference, either in terms of pre-spending directives [making money choices for the child] or by protecting the child from the consequences of their choices, is not real-life and sends the wrong message. Children need practice managing money to become good at it. Let's face it—a financial consequence for a tween who chooses to spend all their money on clothes or candy might be missing out on a movie night with friends. A financial consequence for a young adult who chooses to spend all their money on clothing and clubbing might be serious damage to their credit rating, having phone service terminated, or eviction. Missing a movie night seems like a small price to pay for an invaluable money management life lesson.

By all means, guide your child and offer him words of encouragement. But don't be afraid to let him take risks and watch him fall down. Parents who don't "let go of the handlebars" are depriving their children of the opportunity to learn how to be independent.

• •

Valuable mistakes

When it comes to money, it makes sense that teenagers have a hard time taking the long view. So the only way they can learn financial skills is by being given the opportunity to learn through real experience. It's important, then, that parents resist the urge to control their kids' financial lives. Risks, and the mistakes that come with them, are necessary—so long as parents hold their children accountable … We know that teens who recover from failure are better poised to master their lives. They go further. But they can only recover if they're allowed to fail.—Excerpted from "Want teens to be money savvy? Grab 'em while their brains are getting a tuneup" by Tina Gladstone, *The Globe and Mail*, February 2012

• •

And please, whatever you do, don't come to his rescue when the new *Mario Kart* game loses its novelty appeal and he starts regretting his choice. Allowing him to feel the full effect of his money mistakes will make him that much stronger and resilient down the road, when the financial stakes will be unquestionably higher.

MONEY CAN'T BUY YOU LOVE

We've covered a lot of ground in this chapter, from encouraging your child to try earning an income of his own to the best ways for him to start investing. But although you want your Earning Apprentice to understand the importance of money, you don't want him coming away with any overblown notions that it's the key to a happy life.

Of course, we all need money to survive in today's world. Gone are the days when we lived in caves and could get by without paying rent and by hunting and gathering our own food. Unless you live deep in the wilds of the Amazon rainforest, your kids will have expenses such as a mortgage, food, taxes, clothing, and transportation to worry about when they're older. But how much money is enough? It's a tricky question and one we all have to ask ourselves at some point or another. And it's a good question to pose to your kids as they start earning some of their own money.

We've all heard the saying: *money can't buy happiness.* But in our consumer-driven society, it's hard to escape the notion that money and happiness go hand-in-hand. Advertising campaigns certainly try to sell us (and our kids) on the idea that material possessions are the key to happiness. If you follow this logic, it would make sense that the more money you earn, the more possessions you can own and the happier you'll be. If the current statistics on Canadian personal debt levels are any indication, then as a country we've fallen for this message hook, line, and sinker. But do you really believe it? Certainly there are billionaires in this world who are lonely and miserable. And there are some very happy people who have little more than a roof over their heads. Most of us, however, float somewhere in the middle of these two scenarios and grapple with the daily balancing act of budgeting our needs vs. our wants.

. . . .

Money and happiness

I've been rich and I've been poor. Believe me, honey, rich is better.—*Sophie Tucker*

Vacation season! That's when we find out that money won't buy happiness—but it helps you to look for it in more places.—*Warren Buffett*

I am the richest man in the world, the happiest man in the world.—*King Midas, just before he touched his beloved daughter and she turned into a statue of gold*

. . . .

Undeniably, money can offer a certain measure of comfort and ease ... but can it make us happy? For years, scholars have researched the subject of happiness, hoping to uncover the secret formula for achieving it. Over time, various factors have been identified as being the strongest indicators for happiness. Earning the respect of your peers, having meaningful relationships, and enjoying good health have all been proven to be better gauges for happiness than money. Keep this in mind when you discuss the subject of money with your children. Especially in these harsh economic times, it's worth reminding ourselves, as well as our children, that the most important sources of wealth in this world don't always come from a bank or a stock certificate.

The next time you're sitting around the dinner table, ask your kids this question: "How much money is enough to make a person happy?" And "if our family won the lottery tomorrow, we could buy more stuff, but would we be any happier?" I guarantee they'll have some interesting answers for you.

Believe it or not, you might even be surprised by your own answers.

MAKING IT FUN
Board games

Acquire. It's time to move up from Monopoly to something more complex and intellectually challenging. We recommend a board game called Acquire. It's not a household name and may be difficult to find, but it is worth the effort.

Like Monopoly, Acquire is about building hotels, but that is where the similarity starts and ends. There are no dice and no pieces to move around a board. Luck plays a huge role in Monopoly ("How could you not land on any of my properties!"). But in Acquire, as in chess, intelligence, calculation, and the ability to see ahead several moves are the critical factors in winning.

Acquire was created by Sid Sackson and first published in 1962. It has had a number of iterations over the years, including the replacement of hotels with generic corporate names at one point. The current version, which is based on Mr. Sackson's original concept, is published by Hasbro under the Avalon Hill brand name.

The game is aimed at kids age twelve and older and requires three to six players (four works best). Playing time is about an hour and a half. The idea is to develop hotel chains by placing numbered tiles on a board. On each turn, players are given an opportunity to buy shares in the hotels. The smaller the chain, the cheaper the shares, and some hotel groups are worth more than others (just as in Monopoly, where hotels on Boardwalk and Park Place are worth more than those on Baltic and Mediterranean).

One of the key strategies is to identify which chains are most likely to grow, thereby increasing the value of their stock and the wealth of the player. The tiles a player holds in his hand (six at a time) will help determine where growth is most likely. It's a good idea to delay playing tiles that will expand a chain so that the shares can be purchased at a cheaper price.

Mergers, which occur when a piece is played that joins two separate chains, provide big payoffs to the largest share-holders, thus giving them more money to invest. In the end, the player with the most money (determined by the amount of cash and the value of all shares held) is the winner.

The concept is quite simple to grasp and kids who enjoy games will get into it very quickly. In our experience, there is always a lot of discussion afterwards about moves that could have changed the whole outcome—much like chess.

The major negative is the number of pieces involved. There are 108 tiles, and losing even one can create distortions in the play. There are also 175 stock certificates, plus a supply of money and miscellaneous other pieces.

You probably won't find Acquire at your local game store, but it is available on-line through Amazon.com and various game websites. Copies also are frequently available on eBay. Prices can vary significantly so check before you place an order. Acquire and its creator have a Facebook page at www.facebook.com/SidSackson, but it does not appear to be very active.

On-line games
Kid Review: The Mint

Address: www.themint.org

Sponsors: The Northwestern Mutual Foundation, the charitable arm of Northwestern Mutual, and the National Council on Economic Education (NCEE).

Tab: Fun for kids

Comments: There are four sections under this tab: Earning, Saving, Spending, and Giving. Each has two parts: Discover, which lists facts about money and ways you can be smart with it, and Play, which has quizzes, calculators, and other ways you can play while learning.

Strong points: 1) There are some good tips such as using four jars for your money, one for saving, one for spending, one for investing, and one for giving away.

2) The user interface is nicely conceived with animated navigation buttons that include sound effects.

Weak points: 1) The navigation buttons, while clever, are poorly executed and only work a small percentage of the time. You have to reload the page often to get the buttons to actually send you to the page you're trying to visit.

2) Some of the material has been copy-pasted from the Tips for Tweens section of the site. So the quizzes ask stuff like "Are you satisfied with your current job?" and don't offer an "I don't have a job" option. Another example: "How often do you use your credit card?"—but in the Discover part of that section they talk about how your parent likely has a credit card and you likely don't.

Favourite feature: The Compounding Calculator, the 10 percent of the time *when it actually works.*

Rating: 2/5

Reviewer: Keynen, age thirteen

Buying stock

Playing games with make-believe stock certificates is one thing. Owning shares in a real company is something else again. Once your child reaches a point where he's showing some interest in investing, you might consider giving him a gift of shares for a birthday, Christmas, Hanukkah, or whatever occasion seems appropriate.

Don't pick the stock at random. Choose a company that he knows and has an interest in. Apple (trading symbol AAPL), Google (GOOG), Sony (SWE), McDonald's (MCD), Tim Hortons (THI), Walt Disney (DIS), Coca-Cola (KO), and Mattel (MAT) are examples. However, some of those stocks are very expensive—at the time of writing, both Apple and Google cost more than US$600 per share. So be aware of the price before you make a commitment.

There's also the brokerage commission to consider. Unless you are using a discount broker, the expense of buying a small number of shares may be disproportion-ately high. If you have a full-service broker, see if you can get a special deal for buying your gift.

Alternatively, buy the shares directly from a company that offers a dividend reinvestment plan (DRIP). This cuts out the middleman (the broker) and saves you the commission. Once you've bought the first share, you can continue to purchase more stock from the company, and any dividends can be reinvested as well.

These days, most stocks are owned electronically—you don't receive a share certificate that you can tie up with a bow and present to your kid. But if you buy directly from the company treasury, you will receive a statement showing the number of shares that are being held in a custodial account.

There are some websites such as oneshare.com that offer framed stock certificates of popular companies along with personalized scripts such as "My First Stock." But they are expensive. On a day when a share of Walt Disney was quoted on the New York Stock Exchange at US$46.24, oneshare.com was asking US$177.63 for a framed certif-icate of a single share, including shipping and gift wrapping (you could save $5 by wrapping it yourself). For a little more, you could have purchased four shares of the stock through a broker. However, if you have the money and like the idea of a fancy share certificate, it's an option to consider.

Either way, owning stock in a company could open a whole new window for your child. He'll be able to track daily prices changes on the Internet, download annual reports, receive regular dividend cheques, benefit from stock splits, and more. If the stock turns out to be a big winner, like Apple, the profits will help pay for a college education.

But a word of warning. Not all kids will react the same way. Some couldn't care less—they won't be excited to receive the shares and won't have any interest in learning more about the company or how the stock market works. So give careful thought to your child's interests and how he might react to this type of gift before you make a decision.

Books

Growing Money: A Complete Investing Guide for Kids by Gail Karlitz and Debbie Honig. From banks to bonds, from inflation to the stock market, this investing primer covers all the basics for kids who are eager to do more with their money than simply stash it in a piggy bank. It even explains how to read the financial pages, a challenge many adults have never mastered. Quizzes, worksheets, and interesting facts bring a bit of fun to what can often be a dry subject for kids. There's even a Growing Money Investment Game at the end for young people who are ready to take the first steps toward "growing" their own money.

Kidpreneurs: Young Entrepreneurs with Big Ideas by Adam Toren and Matthew Toren. Glossy pages and colourful graphics bring this motivational book to life for young readers. There's a wealth of great information here on how entrepreneurial-minded kids can start their own businesses—from where to find inspiration, start-up costs, pricing, and advertising, to how to write your own business plan, and more. Our only criticism is that this book waffles a bit on its target reader age—while informative, the "Money on the Internet" section is only appropriate for teenagers, while the connect-the-dot games and quizzes are more suitable for the under-eight crowd. Still, this is a worthwhile read for kids with big ideas.

SUMMING UP

It may seem to be pushing matters to suggest that children in this age group should begin to learn about stocks, bonds, and mutual funds. It's not. Many adults only have the vaguest idea of how these securities work and are fearful of them as a result. Most people are going to need some knowledge of investing in their lives, especially now that more pension plans require participants to make their own investment decisions. Of course, you don't want to force the issue if your child is not yet mature enough to handle these concepts, but you should certainly make the effort.

6
YOUNG ADULTS—
AGES 14–17

· · · · · · · · · · · ·

*Money is something that's hard to get
and easy to lose.*

—DAYLEN, AGE FIFTEEN

GETTING READY

Although there are still a few years left to go before she'll be financially independent, the "real world" is looming ever larger. It's getting down to crunch time, folks. In a few short years, your kid will be thinking about moving out of the house. By that time, she'll *need* to know how to balance a budget, how to avoid bad debt, the difference between "need" and "want," how credit cards work, the importance of saving, the concept of compounding interest, and how to earn a living.

So will she be ready? How much does your kid *really* understand about what's coming? If she's anything like most Canadian teenagers, it's time to take off the rose-coloured glasses and give her a healthy dose of reality.

As we mentioned at the beginning of this book, The National Report Card on Youth Financial Literacy found that 51 percent of Canadian young people in the seventeen-to-twenty age range are already in debt (the average amount being $7,966.27). The survey reported that 14 percent said their debt was tied to a line of credit, 25 percent to credit cards, 69 percent to a student loan. Just over half of those young people with student loans believe they'll be able to pay it off in five years, an expectation that is usually not matched by reality.

As you can imagine, having so many of our young people shouldering debt isn't a good sign. It's especially worrisome when we look at the numbers, which show Canadians are more in debt than ever. Overall, we are carrying more than $1.5 trillion in household debt, according to a 2011 study by the Certified General Accountants Association of Canada, and that number is still rising. Our national debt load has become a major concern of Bank of Canada Governor Mark Carney and Finance Minister Jim Flaherty and has resulted in government action to tighten mortgage lending rules in an effort to prevent people from over-extending themselves.

However, it's important for your child to understand there is a difference between good debt and bad debt, or, as we call it, "constructive" debt and "destructive" debt. Knowing the distinction could save them a lot of problems in the years to come.

UNDERSTANDING DEBT

There are really only two kinds of debt. It all comes down to how the borrowed money is used.

"Constructive debt" represents money borrowed to enhance personal wealth or education. We include mortgages in this category because they make it possible to become a homeowner many years sooner than would be the case if you had to save the full purchase price of a house. Home ownership not only provides one of life's basic needs (shelter) but is a key element of personal wealth, based on the long-term rise in real estate values.

Student loans fall into this category because they enable young people to advance their education, which in turn will improve their earning power. Business loans to launch or expand a company also qualify. However, we have mixed views about the desirability of taking on a student loan, which we will discuss in more depth later in this chapter.

In short, provided it is properly handled, constructive debt can enhance your child's lifestyle and career satisfaction.

"Destructive debt" will have exactly the opposite effect. It will drain away financial assets and lead to anxiety, family conflict, and, in some cases, bankruptcy, with all the hardship that entails. You can recognize this type of debt by applying four criteria:

1. It is incurred for consumption purposes. The money is borrowed to purchase goods or services, not for business, education, or investing purposes.
2. It carries a high interest rate.

3. Servicing the debt requires a disproportionate share of income. In other words, it costs more each month to meet the financing payments than a person is comfortable with.

4. Interest on the debt is not tax deductible.

Your role as a parent is to discourage your youngster from embarking on this slippery slope. That may not be easy. Many teenagers don't consider the future consequences of their actions. They want things now. How they will pay for them later is secondary and if they get into trouble, Mom and Dad will always bail them out, won't they?

Your answer to that has to be "no." You must make your child understand that she is responsible for any expenses that she incurs without your approval. Her greatest temptation will be to get a credit card, which she may believe will open every door at the local mall.

The siren call of credit

Credit card companies are so desperate for new business that they're even going after people who don't exist. We have heard of cases where the families of deceased people have received credit card solicitations for two years or more after the funeral. That's bad enough, but we've also had personal experience with pitches made to people who never walked the earth. Yes, the card companies want their business too!

Gordon explains: A fictitious individual who never lived in our house has received numerous offers from credit card companies over the years saying things like "you are already approved."

How could that happen? Easily! Many years ago, when our children were in their teens and still at home with us, we gave up in despair at ever being able to use the telephone and installed a separate line just for them. Since their first initials were K and D, we had the phone listed in the directory under the name K.D. Pape.

None of the children had that combination of initials in their own full name, so there was no such individual. It was simply a matter of convenience.

K.D. Pape never bought anything, never had a bank account, never applied for credit, and never received mail—that is, until the first credit card offer arrived telling K.D. that he/she/it had been "pre-approved."

To this day, I'm not sure how good old K.D. made it on to some company's direct mail list to be sold to any interested buyer, but I assume the name was simply lifted from the phone book or a city directory.

Of course, we never responded to these solicitations. But they still arrive—in fact, one came in from American Express about the time this was written.

Just to show you how absurd this is, our children are now in their forties and have long since moved out on their own, so this has been going on for more than twenty-five years! Old mailing lists never die, it seems.

This is no isolated example. We've all heard stories about how a dog or a cat received a credit card. Competition for your credit business is fierce, and financial institutions will bend over backwards to win you over.

Politicians and regulators are trying to control some of the more outrageous practices of the card issuers, such as mailing unrequested cheques to card holders, but the industry is still rife with abuses. It's easy to get sucked in and to start running up balances. That's especially true for young people.

. . . .

A nine-year-old's thoughts on credit cards

Let's say you want $1 million on your credit card ... you buy it and you pay them $1 million. Then when you go to the store and want to buy something for $10, they swipe your card and see that you have $1 million and you get to keep what you bought.—Jimmy, age nine

. . . .

Just say no!

These companies want your teen's business—badly! To get it, most financial institutions promote special cards just for students with easy qualifying terms—such as having zero income!

It's somewhat akin to tobacco companies trying to hook high school kids on the habit (which of course they insist they would never do). Get the teens going with a credit card and they'll be customers for life.

The banks try to legitimize their efforts by saying a student card makes it easy to track spending and provides a way to build a credit history at an early age. That may be true, but the potential downside worries us more—the risk that your youngster will acquire a debt habit at an early age and will suffer the consequences for the rest of her life.

So here's our advice if your teen asks, even begs, for her own credit card: just say no! Once she's an adult and on her own, she can make her own decisions about debt, but while she's under your roof enforce a "no cash, no buy" rule.

Kid quote

I don't think I could afford a credit card.—Erin, age seventeen

Of course, if you're up to your neck in credit card debt yourself, that may be difficult to enforce. So before you start lecturing your teen on the subject, make sure your own ledger is clean.

The classic rule for dealing with credit card debt is very simple: don't have any. Pay off your balance in full at the end of each month and you'll never have a problem.

If you already have a balance, the first priority is to reduce the amount of interest you are paying on it. Most mainstream credit cards have an annual rate of about 20 percent. So the first priority for anyone carrying a credit card balance must be to reduce the interest cost and use the money saved to pay off the principal faster.

The cheapest way to do that is to obtain a home equity line of credit. Some financial institutions offer them for as little as prime plus half a percent. If that's not practical, move to a low-interest card as soon as possible. One good source of information on low-interest cards is redflagdeals. com.

Getting back to your teen, what is the alternative if for any reason you can't or won't say no? In that case, you have two options. One is to insist that the card have a credit limit of no more than $500. That allows some spending power for emergency situations without the risk that your teen will go so deeply into debt that it will cause serious financial hardship for her, and you. The other is to use a prepaid credit card. Like retail gift cards, these are pre-loaded with a certain amount of money in advance. Once that is used up, the card becomes valueless until it is reloaded. The concept is similar to a debit card except that this one is not tied to a bank account. Because your teen can never spend more than the pre-loaded amount, she can't go into debt.

FIRST JOB

First steps, first words, first lost tooth—these moments probably feel light years away from the know-it-all teenager living in your home today. By this point, those precious "firsts" in her life are few and far between. But your child's first job is a major milestone. And, just like all the firsts that have come before, she'll need your support and wisdom to navigate this new terrain.

Although employment regulations vary from province to province, by the time she's sixteen, your teen is of legal age to work almost anywhere in Canada (except, for instance, in a mine or at a job that involves serving alcohol). There are many ways she can earn some extra income—maybe she's interested in counselling at a summer camp or working after school at the mall, lifeguarding at a local pool or running games at an amusement park. Even better, if she's achieved her instructors' certificate in a skill such as music or swimming, there's some great money to be earned teaching or tutoring.

Whatever path she chooses, the experience of writing a resumé or filling out an application, preparing for an interview, and presenting herself professionally are invaluable lessons for the "real world" lurking around the corner. Every kid will be ready for her first job at a certain point … some earlier than others. By the time high school graduation rolls along, most Canadian teens will have worked for pay at some point or another. But how do you know when *your* child is ready to start looking for that all-important first job? Here are a few factors you might want to consider.

Reliability: Can you trust her to act responsibly? To be punctual? Is she doing a good job balancing the responsibilities of schoolwork, home life, and friends? Then she might be ready to add a part-time job to her plate right now.

Maturity: Is she mature enough to handle herself professionally in a job situation? Will she be able to take the demands of a job seriously? Is she ready to be spending less time at home and with her friends? Shyness is common among teens—consider whether your child has enough confidence to speak up for herself if she has questions or concerns about the job.

Independence: How self-reliant is she? Does she get herself to school on time in the morning? Does she complete homework and chores without reminders? Can she manage her time effectively? If need be, can she get herself to and from work on her own?

Motivation: Does she *want* a job? Some kids are more ambitious and driven than others. Before she's ready for a job outside the home, your teen has to have the right mindset. If she's dragging her heels and fighting the idea of working outside the home, this might not be the best time to push it. She might not yet be emotionally ready for the responsibility. On the other hand, some kids will certainly be more motivated to make money than others. If she's expected to contribute to the cost of her own post-secondary education, she'll probably want to get a jump-start on saving her money.

. . . .

Wake-up call coming

I'm never going to get a summer job. I work hard in school all year. Summer's my time to relax.—Jonah, age nine (who's in for a big surprise in about five or six years)

. . . .

As parents, we try to do as much as possible for our kids. But landing that first job and earning a paycheque of her own will give your teen a sense of satisfaction, independence, confidence, and pride that you'll never be able to provide her with. No matter where she ends up in her future career, that first job is a rite of passage she'll never forget.

The hunt

So once she's ready, where do you look? It's a good idea to start in your own neighbourhood—the local newspaper, the nearby mall, community centre, park, or swimming pool all might have job openings posted. Alternatively, if you have friends or family who own or operate a business, perhaps they are looking to hire a student for summer or weekend hours. If none of these are options for your teen, there are also some reputable websites that post job listings for youth.

Here's a good starting point: www.youth.gc.ca. Run by the Government of Canada, this website is full of information on youth employment, from writing a resumé to gaining work experience. You can also find links to a national Student Job Bank run by Service Canada.

Be aware of where and how your teen is searching for a job. If she's scrolling through the job postings on Craigslist, it's time to raise the red flags—there are a lot of scam artists out there.

When she does find a job posting that interests her, she might need your help filling out the application. This is the point where any kind of previous work outside the home (babysitting, neighbourhood yard work, etc.) can give your teen an edge in terms of references and experience.

Dress for success

The idea of presenting herself well for that first job interview might come as a shock to your teen. These days, it means more than just wearing the right clothes. Before she heads out the door for the interview, body piercings (beyond earrings) should be taken out (or at the very least, kept to a minimum), tattoos (if she has any) should be covered, hair should be neat (or at the very least, clean), and any under-garments stowed (bra straps for girls, low-hanging pants for boys). Too much skin is definitely not a professional look, so be sure she leaves the short-shorts and spaghetti straps at home. It's worth mentioning that, although the way a person looks should never be a consideration for employment, the reality is that personal appearance has an effect on people, whether they're conscious of it or not. When you're vying for a job, you want as much working in your favour as possible. Looking professional is important.

Appearances aside, the reality is that, unfortunately, these days jobs aren't easy to come by … especially for those poised to enter the work force. At the time of publi-cation, youth unemployment rates were high (Statistics Canada reported a jobless rate of 17.3 percent in June 2012 for youth ages seventeen to nineteen). With so many teens competing for so few positions, your child should be prepared for the fact that she might not get her dream job right away. In fact, this could very well be her first experience with rejection, so it's a good idea to have a conversation with her about the realities of the situation.

To help her chances of landing the job, before she heads off to the interview, encourage her to do a bit of research on the company or organization so she'll be able to speak knowledgeably about it. You might also consider staging a mock job interview at home the day before, so she can get an idea of what to expect when the big moment arrives.

Of course, when she does get that job, keep a close eye on her. If you find that your teen becomes overwhelmed with her new responsibilities, consider paring back the hours until she's more comfortable with her new responsibilities. No job is worth compromising grades, health, or friendships.

THE TAXMAN COMETH

The thrill of earning a paycheque could be tempered if source deductions are withheld to satisfy the taxman. So it's a good idea to prepare your teen in advance and take steps to minimize the impact.

The Canada Revenue Agency (CRA) requires that employers withhold a portion of all salaries at source and remit it to Ottawa every month. The amount will depend on how much your youngster earns. The starting point is what is known as a TD1 form, known as a Personal Tax Credits Return. The employer will give one of these to your teen to complete. Make sure she does it—CRA rules say that, if it isn't done within seven days, a minimum fine of $100 will apply. Although it is doubtful they'd enforce that in the case of a young person just entering the work force, why take the chance?

The form itself is very straightforward. Most high school students will only qualify for the basic personal amount ($10,822 in 2012) and can ignore all the other lines on the first page except for line 13, where the total claim amount has to be filled in.

What really counts are the boxes on page two. The second box is headed "Total income less than total claim amount." Very few high school students are likely to earn more than $10,822 from part-time work. If that's the case, make sure she checks that box, which will exempt her from having any tax withheld at source. Now all she has to do is sign and date the form at the bottom of page two, hand it back to her employer, and she's done.

Canada Pension Plan deductions can also be avoided at this age—they don't kick in until age eighteen. However, young people are not exempt from employment insurance premiums, even though as temporary student workers they would never qualify to make a claim.

Even if your teen does not earn enough money to pay any tax, she should file a return every year. There are several reasons for this. For starters, she may get a few dollars back from an employment insurance overcontribution. Next, her income for that year will be in the CRA's records and will increase her RRSP contribution room, which can be used now or when she is older and is working full time.

Also, it's a good idea to get into the habit of filing a tax return—many college students miss out on claiming the refundable GST/HST credit, which cuts in at age nineteen, because they neglect to file. That can amount to more than $250 a year, so it's worth the trouble.

If you use a tax software program, have your teen prepare her return on it as well. It shouldn't cost any more (most programs allow for the completion of more than one return), and it will familiarize her with what to expect in future years.

OPEN AN RRSP?

Once your teen starts earning income and filing a tax return, she is eligible to open an RRSP. There is no minimum age for having a retirement savings plan, unlike a Tax-Free Savings Account (TFSA) which cannot be opened before age eighteen.

The question is whether an RRSP makes any sense at this stage. The answer, as is so often the case with financial matters, is "it depends."

There are two main advantages to RRSPs. First, you get a tax deduction for the amount you contribute. Second, the money in the plan grows tax-sheltered until it is withdrawn. At that point it becomes taxable income.

The tax deduction part probably won't be of any value to your teen since it is unlikely she will be earning more than the basic personal amount. However, there's a little-known rule that says a deduction does not have to be claimed in the same year a contribution is made—it can be carried forward indefinitely. So if an RRSP contribution is made now, the deduction could be claimed years later when your teen has become an adult and is working full-time.

Tax-free compounding is valuable at any age. But if the return on the invested money is very small, tax sheltering won't be worth much. If your teen contributes $500 and the money is put into a high-interest savings account paying 2 percent, it will only earn $10 a year. That's not enough to make it worthwhile setting up a plan, especially if the intention is to withdraw the money relatively soon.

That said, there are some situations in which opening an RRSP at this stage would be worthwhile. The first is if your teen seriously wants to begin a long-term savings plan. Because of the magic of compounding, the younger a person is when she starts saving and investing, the more her money will grow.

For example, if she contributes $500 to an RRSP at age fifteen and earns an average of 5 percent annually over the years, she'll have $5,734 at age sixty-five, even if she never contributes another penny. By contrast, the same $500 contributed at age twenty-five would only grow to $3,520 at sixty-five. Those early years can really add up.

For an even more dramatic illustration, suppose she contributed $500 *every* year from age fifteen on. By age sixty-five her RRSP would be worth $115,641. By doing the same thing from age twenty-five, her plan would be worth only $66,940 or 42 percent less.

It's also worth keeping in mind that the money does not have to be used only for retirement, which will seem like a pretty vague and distant concept to your teen. When she's older, she can take an RRSP loan of up to $25,000 to buy her first house or condo using the Home Buyers' Plan.

An RRSP can also be used as a source of funds for post-secondary education. Several years ago, the federal government launched a program called the Lifelong Learning Plan. It allows tax-free withdrawals, in the form of RRSP loans, to a maximum of $20,000 to pay for a college education.

The rules do not allow parents to use this program on behalf of their children. But if your teen has her own RRSP, she can take advantage of it when the time comes to go on to college or university.

RRSP rules limit annual contributions to 18 percent of earned income. That doesn't add up to a lot for a young person working part-time but let's suppose your teen is able to earn $2,000 over a year. This means she can contribute $360 a year to an RRSP. If she starts at age sixteen and the money earns an average of 5 percent annually, she will have $2,067 at age twenty.

At that point, she would have two choices. She could use the Lifelong Learning Plan to borrow the money from her RRSP to help pay for her first year of college. She has ten years after finishing her courses to repay the money, interest-free.

Alternatively, she could simply close the RRSP and withdraw the cash. Although the withdrawal would be taxable income, if she is not earning very much, that won't matter because she will still fall well short of the basic personal amount. However, ask if there is a closing fee for terminating the account before proceeding.

Where to invest?

If your teen decides to open an RRSP, how should the money be invested? As we saw earlier, putting it into something like a high-interest savings account makes no sense in terms of tax saving. If that's what she wants to do, forget about the RRSP.

Instead, she should be looking for an investment that will provide a decent return at no cost and with relatively low risk. The best way to achieve this is by opening a mutual fund RRSP at a bank or other financial institution. There may be a small set-up fee for doing this, although that might be waived if she uses the same bank at which you normally do business. There should be no annual administration fee if the plan invests in the bank's own mutual funds, but ask first. Also ask what the minimum investment requirement is for mutual funds. Typically it is $500, but many financial institutions offer a reduced minimum for RRSPs.

Bank mutual funds can be purchased on a no-load basis. That means she won't have to pay any sales commission. Since she won't have a lot of money to invest at the outset, this is a major plus.

Our advice is to invest in a low-risk Canadian neutral balanced fund to start with. These funds offer a combi- nation of stocks (usually about 50 to 60 percent of the portfolio) and bonds. They are not risk-free, but if she asks the bank advisor for a low-volatility fund, the chances of losing money over time are low. Over the ten years to the end of May 2012, the average fund of this type gained 5.35 percent annually. And remember, this includes the market crash of 2008–09.

As long as the fund performs well, she won't need to go beyond it for the first few years. Once she is out of college and ready to invest more money, she can look at diversifying, but that is down the road.

SAVING FOR UNIVERSITY

This is the time when your teen will start to think seriously about what she wants to do with her life. In many cases, that means focusing on post-secondary education.

Of course, *you've* been thinking about this for years, perhaps since before she was born, and wondering where the money was going to come from to pay for it all. If you had foresight, you opened a Registered Education Savings Plan (RESP) many years ago, but unless you have made some very large contributions, it probably has nowhere near enough money to finance a college degree.

Those costs can range from expensive to overwhelming, depending on the type and length of the degree and whether the student goes out of town. For example, a Toronto student attending Ryerson Polytechnic University and living at home can expect to pay about $6,200 a year just for tuition and books, according to the University Cost and

Debt Calculator on the Get Smarter About Money website of the Investor Education Fund. That's almost $25,000 to earn a four-year degree, and those costs don't include transportation, food, entertainment, personal effects, and incidentals.

The costs escalate dramatically for the student who has her heart set on going away to a glamorous school and living in residence. A four-year engineering degree at the University of British Columbia will cost an out-of-town student more than $16,000 a year or $64,000+ by the time the parchment is handed out. If your kid wants to be a doctor, be prepared to re-mortgage the house. Four years of medical school at Ontario's prestigious Queen's University will set her, and you, back by more than $108,000.

So where will the money come from? The first step is to have a serious conversation with your teen about the future. The goal is to get her thinking realistically about what lies ahead. She may dream of going off with her friends to Western, but maybe it's an impossible dream once the numbers are crunched. If you have to squelch the idea, better to do it now than later.

The conversation must include a hard-nosed look at who is going to pay for what. Unless you are very wealthy or have been very disciplined with your education savings, you probably won't be able to pay the whole shot yourself. This will be especially true if there is more than one child to consider. So lay it all on the table. Tell her that she must assume part of the responsibility for paying the bills.

One approach is to say that you'll pay for the basics—tuition and books. The rest is up to her. If she wants to go away to university, she has to pay for residence, meals, transportation, etc. This puts the onus on her to make practical decisions. Once she looks at the expenses involved in living away from home, she may have a different view on the whole idea.

It's important not to take a dogmatic position. You may feel that having her continue to live at home while attending a nearby school makes the most financial sense. But if she has her heart set on going out of town and having more independence, there's a serious risk of escalating tension and even alienation if you push too hard.

Take a conciliatory approach instead. Tell her you support her dream and will do everything you can to help her make it happen—short of paying for it yourself. It's *her* dream, after all. If she really wants it to come true, make sure she understands she has to contribute to it.

One way to help is to explore with her the many financial options available. For example, have her download information about the scholarships and bursaries available at the schools in which she is interested. Go over them in depth with her, and help her identify those for which she might qualify.

For example, the University of Toronto offers approximately 2,400 scholarships with a value of more than $5.2 million. In 2010–11, Montreal's McGill University awarded entrance scholarships worth $2.7 million to 800 students. The University of British Columbia offers more than ninety major entrance scholarships a year to Canadian secondary school students with values ranging from $5,000 to $40,000. There's a lot of money out there!

. . . .

Scholarship success

What's important in the scholarship game is to make yourself a strong candidate well before it comes time to actually apply for scholarship money. Many scholarships now look at more than just marks, including such criteria as leadership skills, community involvement and initiative, and volunteer roles. Therefore, get involved while in high school: take on leadership roles, get involved through volunteering in the community and participating in extracurricular and athletic activities. When it comes time to apply at the end of high school, it will expand the number of scholarships that you are able to apply for and make you a much more competitive scholarship candidate.
—Murray Baker, author of *The Debt Free Graduate: How to Survive College or University Without Going Broke*

. . . .

Some scholarships have very specialized requirements. The University of Toronto has one that is open only for black students in financial need, another that is available exclusively to female residents of Etobicoke, one for Native students in health profession programs, one for a student with a particular interest in Canada–Japan relations, and more. Obviously, only a limited number of people will qualify for these focused awards, so if your teen is eligible, her chances will be much improved. Information on all scholarships, bursaries, and awards can be found on the institutions' websites.

There are also scholarships available from a wide range of organizations including the Girl Guides of Canada, TD Canada Trust, and the Canadian Millennium Foundation. And don't overlook the Canada Student Grants Program, which is operated by the federal government. It doesn't offer big money, but payments of up to $2,000 a year are available to students from low- and middle-income families as well as disabled students and those with dependents.

Even if your teen gets a grant or scholarship, she may wish to work during the summer and perhaps part-time during the school year to earn some extra money to put toward her college savings. Go over the possibilities with her, and help her estimate how much she might reasonably be able to put aside. Remind her that once she starts college or university, her summer earning power will increase as most schools finish all courses and exams by the end of April, giving students four months off.

College without debt

The best book we've seen on paying for a college education is *The Debt Free Graduate* written by Murray Baker. Now in its twelfth edition since it was first published in 1996, it has sold more than 175,000 copies. If your bookstore doesn't have it, go to www.debtfreegrad.com.

If there still isn't enough money available, she may want to consider a student loan. They are available from a number of sources, public and private. The federal government's Canada Student Loans Program works in partnership with most provinces and territories to provide 60 percent of the assessed need, up to a maximum of $210 per week of study. The remaining 40 percent may be provided in the form of provincial or territorial student loans. An estimated 4.3 million students have received almost $32 billion in Canada Student Loans since the program was created in 1964. For more details, search for Canada Student Loans and Grants in the Human Resources and Skills Development Canada website.

The provinces have their own programs, and many students have come to rely on them for support. The biggest is the Ontario Student Assistance Program (OSAP) which offers a loan/grant combination of up to $12,240 per academic year, of which only $7,300 is repayable. The loans are interest free for as long as the student is studying and for six months after. Interest charges after that are tax deductible. You can find a list of all provincial and territorial student loan websites at https://you.ubc.ca/ubc/vancouver/cdnloans.ezc.

Note that in some provinces (Alberta, Manitoba, Nova Scotia, and Prince Edward Island) Canada Student Loans are available alongside any provincial assistance. In Saskatchewan, Ontario, New Brunswick, Newfoundland and Labrador, and British Columbia they are integrated into the provincial programs. Canada Student Loans are not available in Quebec, the Northwest Territories, and Nunavut—those jurisdictions have their own programs. In Yukon, only Canada Student Loans are available to full-time residents.

The upside of a student loan is that it gives your young person an opportunity to earn a post-secondary degree that might otherwise have been financially out of reach. The downside, of course, is that it is expected to be repaid. The terms are lenient, but the inescapable fact is that the graduate is left carrying what could be tens of thousands of dollars in debt at the very start of her working life. That burden could take many years to pay off. Therefore, our advice is to explore every other option before going the student loan route.

Handouts don't help

It's understandable that you want to help your children succeed in life. But handouts are not the way to do it. In the international bestseller *The Millionaire Next Door*, author Thomas Stanley says studies show that adults who receive generous financial support from their parents usually end up with less wealth than those who don't receive any assistance, taking income brackets into account. His conclusion is that financial handouts, however well-intentioned, inhibit a person's ability to create wealth.

JUNIOR ENTREPRENEURS

Entrepreneurship is one of Canada's greatest strengths.
—Stephen Ashworth, President and CEO (Acting) of Junior Achievement Canada

We were young, but we had good advice and good ideas and lots of enthusiasm.—Bill Gates, co-founder of Microsoft Corporation

With jobs so scarce these days, many teens are scrambling to find ways to make extra income … especially those who need to fund some or all of their own post-secondary education. Unfortunately, some are getting frustrated and backing out of the job market entirely. Others are turning to the idea of entrepreneurship. After all, if you can't find a job, why not create one for yourself? As they say, necessity is the mother of invention. And young people, with their natural resilience and seemingly unlimited reserves of energy and enthusiasm, are uniquely suited to take on new ventures.

There are certainly some famous success stories out there—Bill Gates and Richard Branson were both teenage entrepreneurs. And Mark Zuckerberg of Facebook fame is perhaps the most well-known young entrepreneur of all time. On the Canadian front, you might have heard about Toronto native and junior entrepreneur Michael Furdyk, who co-founded his on-line technology business—MyDesktop.com—in his early teens. By the time Furdyk had reached the tender age of seventeen, the business was thriving and later that year sold for a million-dollar price tag. He followed it up with BuyBuddy.com, his second on-line business. Now thirty, his current enterprise, TakingITGlobal, promotes awareness and engagement among global youth.

Not too shabby, eh?

But your kid doesn't necessarily have to be aiming to make a fortune with her business. Perhaps she just wants to earn enough to buy a laptop or help fund her tuition fees. Or perhaps she's identified a need in a certain market that she wants to fill.

. . . .

Money quote

I don't go into ventures to make a fortune. I do it because I'm not satisfied with the way others are doing business.
—Richard Branson, former teen entrepreneur

. . . .

The worm king

Sometimes a young person's entrepreneurial instincts can take an unexpected turn. Here's what happened to Gordon when he was young:

I grew up in the Michigan countryside. Directly across from our house was a body of water that was too big to call a pond and too small to have lake status. We referred to it as "the bayou." The bayou teemed with fish at that time (the 1940s). From the time I was four years old, I would be down there most days in the summer catching sunfish, bluegills, rock bass, perch, dogfish, and—the big thrill—black bass. It was my own private fishing hole—most of the time there was no one there but me.

That changed after the end of the Second World War and the end of gas rationing in the United States. Some people from the city of Muskegon, about twenty-five miles away, discovered the bayou offered some easy meals and started coming on weekends. Soon the banks were lined with fishermen (and women), most using bamboo poles and whatever bait they could scrounge—crickets, grasshoppers, and the like.

I saw an opportunity. I knew from experience that the bayou fish preferred worms above all else—especially worms from the big compost pile on our property, where all the grass cutting and leaf rakings had been dumped for years. I got some empty tin cans from my mother, grabbed a shovel, and went to work.

Talk about easy money! I sold the worms for a dime a dozen, and I couldn't dig them fast enough to meet the demand. Before long, I raised the price to fifteen cents and then to a quarter. The demand didn't drop off—the worms did the job and there was no competition. During a typical summer weekend, I could earn between five and ten dollars—a fortune in those days when a Coke cost a nickel. I had identified a need that no one else was meeting and I fulfilled it at a reasonable price—the classic formula for entrepreneurial success.

Epilogue: When I returned to Michigan many years later, the bayou had been badly polluted by industrial waste from a chemical plant upstream. The water surface was covered with green algae. There were no fish.

Giving support

Whatever your teen's goal, if she's got a business idea she's dying to try out, be sure to give her your support and encouragement. Here are some things to consider.

Is my kid entrepreneur material? Entrepreneurship is the meeting point between business and creativity. If your teen isn't afraid to try new things, take a risk, and put a lot of time and work into a business venture, entrepreneurship could be something she might want to consider. Stephen Ashworth, president and CEO (acting) of Junior Achievement Canada, says, "Young entrepreneurs must have a high level of passion, commitment, curiosity, and self-confidence. They must embrace innovative and creative thinking and thrive in a dynamic and ever-changing world."

What can I, as a parent, do to help? Even if you have no business background to speak of, there's a lot you can do to support your junior entrepreneur. For starters, give her the freedom and encouragement to try. After all, as Wayne Gretzky once famously said, "You miss 100 percent of the shots you don't take."

If your teen comes to you for help, offer your guidance (without taking over the project). According to Stephen Ashworth, "Parents can support their children's entrepreneurial spirit by allowing them to discover the risk and rewards of starting a business." If your teen is still in the brainstorming stage, encourage her to consider starting her business in an area she's passionate about. Remember, it should be fun. If her heart isn't in it, she won't end up giving it her all. Does she love animals? Then perhaps she might want to start up a pet-sitting business or dog-walking business (you would be amazed at the amount of money dog walkers can make). Is she a computer whiz? What about a neighbourhood tech-support service? Does she have a green thumb? How about a landscaping/gardening business? Weeding neighbours' gardens once a week could be quite lucrative.

There's a lot involved with creating a business from scratch. Your teen also might appreciate some help writing a business plan, calculating start-up costs, and figuring out how to tackle advertising and promotion. There are also websites that offer advice and information for kids and parents. Here are a couple of them to get you going:

www.raisingceokids.com
www.youngentrepreneur.com

Probably the best place to go for support is Junior Achievement Canada. JA is a non-profit organization dedicated to inspiring and preparing youth to succeed in a global economy. Run by volunteer business professionals and mentors, JA programs are free of charge and available to young people across Canada. For more information, check out www.jacan.org.

· ·

What JA can do

Junior Achievement helps to cultivate the entrepreneurial spirit. A recent independent Boston Consulting Group study completed to assess the impact of Junior Achievement's mission showed that 70 percent of Achievers indicate that participation in a Junior Achievement of Canada program had a significant impact on their desire to be an entrepreneur. It also showed that Junior Achievers are 50 percent more likely to open their own business which leads to innovation, new jobs, and wealth creation. In fact, JA alumni launch 6,500 companies a year, at a rate 50 percent higher than the Canadian average. —Stephen Ashworth, president and CEO (acting) of Junior Achievement Canada

· ·

MAKING IT FUN
Books

The Motley Fool Investment Guide for Teens: 8 Steps to Having More Money Than Your Parents Ever Dreamed Of by David Gardner, Tom Gardner, and Selena Maranjian. Did that title catch your eye? This is an investment book directly targeted at teens with lots of useful tips from young people themselves. Although it is written from an American point of view and is a bit dated (2002), the information and strategies are still quite relevant today. Topics covered include investments, savings, summer jobs, and the stock market. Personal anecdotes, quotations, and words of advice from money-smart teens make this book an easy-to-read introduction for novice investors—of any age.

Think & Grow Rich by Napoleon Hill. First published in 1937, this book effectively pioneered the financial self-help literary genre. It's become a classic, for good reason. The main message is a simple one: in order to get ahead and succeed, you need desire, determination, and motivation. Although not specifically written for teens, the book is a perfect choice for young people who are starting to think about what to do with their life and how to achieve their goals. Typical quote—"If you do not see great riches in your imagination, you will never see them in your bank balance." An old book, yes, but the messages resonate just as loudly as ever.

Rich Dad, Poor Dad for Teens by Robert T. Kiyosaki. Reminiscent in tone to *The Wealthy Barber*, this book talks to teens about the importance of having the right attitude about money if they want to get ahead. There's a helpful section about teaching financial literacy with examples of how liabilities and assets work for you and boost your savings. This book also explores the concept of games, specifically Monopoly, and how they can play an important role in your attitude toward making money.

Note: If you order the abridged version of this book on-line, don't be surprised when it arrives in the mail. This is a little book—so little, you might miss it at the bottom of the FedEx package. But it gets to the point without mincing words.

How Not to Move Back with Your Parents: The Young Person's Guide to Financial Empowerment by Rob Carrick. This well-written book is a must-read for all young people and their parents. Rob Carrick explores the financial realities facing youth in today's world and the impact on them of coping with monetary burdens they have not been prepared for and may never have imagined, such as paying for post-secondary education. Mr. Carrick also deals with such life-altering topics as moving back in with parents and, later, weddings and children. On the financial side, topics include savings vehicles, debts, budget management, mortgages, banks, and retirement savings.

The book is an eye-opener as it offers explanations and solutions as to why what worked for parents over twenty years ago cannot work today. This is mainly due to increases in the cost of living and the rise in tuition fees, which have gone up at an average rate of 5.6 percent annually since the 1980s, faster than the rate of inflation.

The author also focuses on some of the money trends people of all ages will face in the future, such as cheques being replaced by e-transfers, which of course is already happening. The book also explores such new concepts as the "anti-dowry"—debts people bring to marriages. Mr. Carrick warns that unless young people in the twenty to thirty age group don't develop know-how quickly, they run the risk of being in worse financial shape than their parents, with no money to save for their dreams or retirement.

There are some important issues that the book does not cover such as the often overlooked costs incurred by parents whose children go away to college: moving, keeping in touch by cellphone, or extra money for meal plans or courses. Nor does it cover some of the pitfalls of money transfers or banking by iPhone.

But overall, this book offers some useful advice for parents and their children. Our suggestion to parents of young people in this age group is to read it first and then leave it around for the kids to discover "by accident."

On-line games
Kid review: Financial Soccer
Address: www.financialsoccer.ca

Sponsor: Visa

Comments: There are several national versions of this game available. I played the Canadian edition, but there are also versions for countries from all over the world, from Brazil to China. Those for nations outside North America are called Financial Football, the name for soccer in most parts of the world.

There are three levels of play: Amateur (ages 11–14), Semi-Pro (14–18), and World Class (18+). The goal is to try to win by answering questions relating to money, finance, and credit.

The game is really designed for teachers to use as a way to help educate students about these subjects. Once the game is launched, the player is asked to click on a tab titled "pregame," which brings up a series of educational modules. The first page of module one includes a paragraph that is enough to send most kids surfing for something a little less intimidating: "The following curriculum is intended as a week-long program. Before you play the game, we recommend reviewing and completing the four 45-minute educational modules with your students to help them get a jump on the financial concepts the game covers."

That sounds scary, so it might be a good idea just to ignore the pregame stage and go right to game itself. The first time I played, I chose the single-player version and went to the first level without reading any of the practice notes beforehand, so I went in blind. I got along just fine.

The graphics are good. The game is played in an arena with computerized players. To begin, you choose your country's team (Canada) and an opponent (I picked the United States). You can decide how long you want to play; the shortest game is five minutes. The players kick the ball as in a real soccer game, but there is a pause in the action every few seconds and you are asked to choose if you want to answer an easy, medium, or hard multiple-choice question. The harder the question, the more your team benefits if you get it right. Once you decide, the question pops up, and you are given a certain amount of time to answer. If you get it wrong or take too long to find the right answer, your team may lose the ball through a steal or out-of-bounds.

When you get a chance to take a shot, the question will be a little harder. If you get it right, your player will score; otherwise, the goalie makes a save. If the game is tied at the end, there is a shootout that is decided by answering a series of true/false questions.

I found the game a little hard at the start, because I knew nothing about what I was doing. But I quickly mastered the first level, because it is mostly common sense.

After I finished the first level at ten minutes, I skimmed through the other levels, and they were more difficult. You really need an understanding of money to do well there.

When I played the hardest level (World Class) I really understood how much more difficult it was. For example, at the Amateur level you may get a question like "For four hours work, what is the difference between being paid $5 an hour and $7.50 an hour?" At the World Class level you may be asked to define a HELOC or explain what a student origination loan is.

Strong points: The graphics are good, although they become repetitious after a while. The coding is very effective because the longer you take to get a correct answer, the worse it is for your team and the chances are you will lose the ball. Some of the questions are interesting.

Weak points: Pop-up videos appear occasionally and there was no option to get rid of them. The crowd noise gets annoying after a while—an on/off switch would be good.

Favourite feature: You learn some things about finance in an entertaining way.

Rating: 2.5/5. It was entertaining at the start but I got bored after a little while. Some upbeat music for teens would help.

Reviewer: Michael, age sixteen

Videos

From buying your first car to tracking your spending, www.getsmarteraboutmoney.ca offers "Funny Money" video tutorials for young people. Go to Tools and Calculators and click on Videos.

SUMMING UP

If everything has gone according to plan, your child—now a young adult—is ready for the world. She has held a job, learned to avoid destructive debt, planned for college or university, and started an investment program. You've done your job well. Sit back and relax (if that is ever possible with kids!).

7
THE QUESTIONS KIDS ASK!

*Why doesn't money grow on trees and bushes,
because I think it should?*

—LILY, AGE EIGHT

We wanted to know what children were wondering about money, so we invited the kids at Camp Wahanowin on Ontario's Lake Couchiching, near Orillia, to tell us what was on their mind. We also got some questions from our children, grandchildren, nieces, nephews, and the children of friends. We were surprised, and you may be too, at the sophistication of some of the questions and what they revealed about what kids already know and don't know.

These are questions your own children may ask you at some point (if they haven't already). After reading Gordon's answers, you'll be ready for them!

Q: Why is money made out of trees? —Dylon, age six

A: It won't be for much longer. The old Canadian bills were made of paper which, yes, comes from trees. But we are quickly getting rid of them. Our $20, $50, and $100 notes are now made out of a type of plastic, called polymer. By the end of 2013, the $5 and $10 bills will be too. The old and new bills will circulate side by side for a while but before long the old paper bills will disappear.

The Bank of Canada, which is responsible for producing the bills for our country, says the polymer money will last at least 2.5 times longer than the old paper bills before they wear out. That will save the government some money because it won't have to print new ones as often. The Bank also says the new bills will be harder for criminals to duplicate—that's called *counterfeiting*, and there was starting to be too much of it.

Ask your mom or dad to let you feel one of the new bills and compare it to an old paper one. You'll find it feels much smoother and slicker. It also looks cleaner.

Q: What happens if you run out of money in your bank? —Dahlia, age six

A: To put it simply, the bank won't allow you to withdraw money you don't have. You won't be able to go to a teller or an ATM machine and get cash. You won't be able to use a debit card. Any cheques that you write will be rejected and returned to you, and you'll have to pay a fee of perhaps $25. If you don't do something quickly to get more money into the account, the bank may close it. It's a serious situation.

People who have budgets are unlikely to run out of money, which is why we think a budget is very important. If you receive an allowance, try making one for yourself. Write down on a piece of paper how much you get each week or month, then plan how much you will save and what you will spend it on. That's your budget. As long as you don't go over it, you won't run out of money.

Q: What should I do with my money? Should I spend it all or save a bit? —*Dara, age six*

A: It's always a good idea to save some of your money. You may want to buy something special some time, and if you have some saved money available, you won't have to wait. We suggest you begin by saving twenty-five cents of every dollar you receive. You'll be surprised how quickly it will add up.

Q: How do you pay for things with a credit card? There's no money on it ... or is there? —*George, age six*

A: Each time you use a card, the company that issued it makes a record of the purchase. At the end of every month, they send you a bill for the total amount. You can pay it all or just part. But if you only pay part of the bill, the credit card company will charge interest on the amount that is left, and that can be very expensive—typically around 20 percent a year. That's twenty cents on every dollar! Some people make the mistake of carrying a large unpaid balance on their credit card. That can cost hundreds of dollars in interest each year.

There is money on the card—it's called the credit limit. People are allowed to spend up to that limit but no more. If they exceed it, the card company will refuse to accept any purchase.

Q: Why did they take away the penny?
—Charlotte, age seven

A: Actually, it hasn't gone away, Charlotte. In fact, pennies will probably be in use until you're a grown-up and maybe longer. They just aren't going to make any more. The Royal Canadian Mint, which is responsible for making all our coins, says the penny had just gotten too expensive. It was costing more to make each penny—1.6 cents—than it was worth. That may not seem like much, but it added up to $11 million a year, which is a lot of money. For that cost, the Royal Canadian Mint made almost 663 million pennies in 2011.

Another problem is that the penny will no longer buy anything on its own. It has steadily lost value over the many years it has been around because of something called inflation, which is a gradual increase in the cost of things. Today's penny is only worth one-twentieth of what it was a hundred or so years ago. Since it can't buy anything anymore, some people think it has become a nuisance.

The Mint says people can keep using pennies for as long as they want, and banks will still change your pennies for coins and bills of greater value. So don't stop saving them. In July 2012, a man in the United States paid off his mortgage with 62,000 pennies. It took the bank two days to count them. That proves that if you collect enough of them, they are still worth something.

Q: If you have a lot of money, should you use it on one big thing or lots of little things?
—Jenna, age eight

A: One big thing is usually better. Here's why. A lot of little things won't seem to be worth very much to you. Depending on what you buy, they'll probably get lost, or broken, or eaten, or you'll get tired of them quickly. But if you buy one big thing that you really, *really* need or want, you'll treasure it. It might be a favourite doll, a computer game, or a musical instrument—if it is something that you have decided is important to you, it will be worth a lot more than a bunch of things you really don't care about.

Grown-ups spend their money that way. They place a lot more value on buying big things like a car or even a house. Of course, you're too young to buy a car, but the idea is the same.

Q: **Why doesn't money grow on trees and bushes, because I think it should?**
   —Lily, age eight

A: I think you're kidding us, Lily. You know very well that money could never grow on trees. But what if it did? It wouldn't be a good thing because everyone would have as much as they wanted to pick. That would mean that money would have no value. If you had a money tree in your back yard, why would you want to take money from someone else to pay for work you do for them? It would be like someone offering you five leaves to mow their lawn. Would you do that work for five leaves? Probably not.

Q: **Why did they create money? And why is it called money?** *—Alexa, age eight*

A: You may find this hard to believe but the oldest form of "money" is livestock—cows, sheep, camels, goats, and the like. From about 9000 BC to 6000 BC, this was the most common way of paying for goods. Later, various types of crops were used.

But it's not easy to carry a few cows around in your pocket, so around 1200 BC, the people of China began to use cowrie shells as a way to buy what they wanted. Cowries are found in shallow water in the Pacific and Indian oceans, and many societies have used them as a form of money over the years.

In about 1000 BC, the Chinese went the next step by using bronze and copper to make imitation cowries that were used as substitutes for the real shells. These eventually evolved into coins around 700 BC. The first people in the Western world to use coins were the Lydians, who lived in what is now Turkey, according to the Federal Reserve Bank of Minneapolis.

Paper money came much later. The Bank says the Chinese were the first to use it during the T'ang Dynasty, which lasted from 618 to 907 AD.

The origin of the word *money* is not clear but some historians believe it comes from the Roman temple to Juno, Moneta, where the first coins were made in ancient Rome.

Q: Why do parents get more money than kids?
—Billy, age eight

A: Most money is earned by working. Your mom or dad (maybe both) probably have jobs they go to every day. They get paid for that work, and they may share some of that money with you by giving you an allowance. While they're working, you go to school, play with your friends, or maybe watch TV. You don't get paid for any of those things. Someday, when you have finished school, you'll go to work too and earn some money. But right now, your parents do that and use the money they earn to buy food, make sure you have a place to live, drive a car, and a lot more. They may sometimes think that you have the better deal.

Q: Why do you have to pay to go to university? Why don't the taxes pay for it like regular school? —Jonah, age nine

A: Some people think that college and university should be free. The problem is that it would cost a lot of money, and that would mean raising everyone's taxes. Since many Canadians think their taxes are already too high, that would not be very popular.

But things could change by the time you're ready for university. A lot of work has been done in providing college courses on-line that anyone can take. These could be much less expensive than actually going to the school since one professor could teach many more people and no actual classroom space would be needed. There have been suggestions that these courses might even be free, perhaps with sponsorship from big companies.

Q: What happens if the bank steals some of your money? —Abby, age ten

A: A bank would never steal your money but a bad bank employee might. If that were to happen, the bank would replace any money you lost. If a bank should run into serious financial trouble, your account would be protected for up to $100,000 by the Canada Deposit Insurance Corporation (CDIC). Depositors in some small Canadian banks and trust companies have had to rely on the CDIC to get their money back in the past when the company went bankrupt.

Q: **What is a debit card? How do you put money on a debit card?** —*Charley, age ten*

A: It's a plastic card that you can use to withdraw money from your bank account when you want to buy something. Instead of carrying cash, you give the merchant a debit card and as long as you have enough money in your account, you can buy the item. If you don't have the money, the bank won't allow the payment to go through.

The only way to put money on a debit card is to deposit more money into your bank account.

Many banks offer special accounts for kids that include a debit card, so it is important that you understand how to use it.

Q: **Why is a dime smaller than a penny if it is worth more?** —*Jayda, age ten*

A: Dimes used to be made almost entirely of silver, which is a precious metal. According to the Royal Canadian Mint, until 1919 the dime was 92.5 percent silver, so it was only made as large as that amount of silver would buy. In 1920, the amount of silver was reduced to 80 percent, and it stayed that way until 1967. At that point, it was decided that silver had become too expensive, and from then until 1999 dimes were made of the metal nickel. When even that became too costly, the government switched to the current composition: 92 percent steel, 5.5 percent copper, and 2.5 percent nickel.

If you want to have some fun, ask your parents to give you all their dimes and look through them to see if you can find any that were made before 1968. They're worth a lot more than ten cents because of the amount of silver they contain. In mid-2012, a dime made between 1920 and 1967 had $1.64 worth of silver in it.

You may also be interested to know that old nickels were mostly made of silver, right up until 1942, so those coins are also valuable for their metal content. Today, nickels aren't even made out of nickel, except for a small amount of plating. They are mostly made of steel.

Q: Why are the one- and two-dollar bills in Canada gone? —*Jillian, age eleven*

A: I'm surprised that you asked this question because the bills disappeared long before you were born. Here's what happened. In 1987, the Government of Canada decided that printing dollar bills had become too expensive and decided to replace them with a coin (which we call the "loonie") because it would last much longer. Some people were against the idea because it meant carrying more heavy change in their pockets, but the plan went ahead and dollar bills were withdrawn from circulation in 1989.

A few years later, in 1996, the two-dollar bill was also withdrawn and replaced by the coin with the polar bear on the back that we know as the "toonie" or "twonie."

Q: Why don't we have half-dollars anymore?
—*Rebecca, age eleven*

A: Actually, we do. You just don't see many of them because they are not popular and the Mint makes very few of them. In 2010, only 150,000 half-dollars were struck compared to 167.5 million quarters. The back of the fifty-cent coin shows the Canadian coat of arms, which honours this country's four founding nations: England, Scotland, Ireland, and France.

If you should find any half-dollars dated before 1968, hang on to them. They are made mostly of silver and worth a lot of money. In July 2012, the meltdown value of those coins was $8.18.

Q: Would society be better off without money and instead barter and trade?
—*Oliver, age twelve*

A: We tried that thousands of years ago. It didn't work out too well, which is why money was invented in the first place. One problem with bartering is that there is no general agreement on what is fair value. What is a kilogram of tomatoes worth? A lot depends on how much you like tomatoes.

Let's think about this in real-life terms. Suppose you want a new iPod. If there were no money, you'd have to offer the man who sells them something that he would think is fair value. What would that be? Perhaps you could offer to walk his dog every day for three months. Maybe he'll like the idea but think that three months isn't enough and suggest five months, twice a day. Is that fair? Who knows? It's for you and him to decide.

Now just imagine those same negotiations going on every time someone wanted to buy something. The world of commerce would grind to a halt. Money is the grease that makes all the wheels turn because it has a specific value that everyone can agree on. Not only that, but it allows you to shop around to see if you are getting a fair deal. Imagine going on the Internet and trying to compare iPod prices if we used a barter system. It would be impossible.

Q: **Can money become useless?**
   —Orly, age twelve

A: Yes, it can. It happens when something called hyperinflation occurs in a country. Prices rise at a crazy rate, and your money buys less and less as each hour goes by.

The worst example in history was in the Eastern European country of Hungary in 1945–46, right after the end of the Second World War. It got so bad that at one point prices were doubling every fifteen hours. To keep up, the government kept issuing new paper money of higher and higher denominations. For example, in 1944, the largest banknote was the 1,000 pengő, the Hungarian currency at the time. By mid-1946, it had reached 100,000,000,000,000,000,000 pengő, a figure we can't even imagine. People had to carry their money in wheelbarrows just to buy one loaf of bread. According to Wikipedia, when the government finally replaced the pengő in August 1946 with a new currency called the forint, the total value of all Hungarian banknotes in circulation amounted to 1/1,000 of one US dollar.

Fortunately, we have never experienced hyperinflation in Canada. But there was a case in the United States during the Civil War. The breakaway Southern states issued their own currency, called Confederate dollars. As the war dragged on and it became increasingly apparent the South would lose, Confederate dollars steadily lost value until at the end they were virtually worthless.

Q: What is the return rate on stocks and bonds in Canada?—Shane, age twelve

A: It depends on what time frame you're looking at. A table on the website taxtips.ca shows that, over the twenty years to the end of 2011, the Canadian stock market gained an average of 6.2 percent annually. If you had invested $1,000 at the start of that period, it would have been worth $3,324 at the end. However, if you look at shorter-term numbers, the results are not as good. Over the previous five years, which included the crash of 2008–09, the average annual rate of return from stocks was –1.7 percent.

Bonds are a different story. Over a twenty-year period, Government of Canada bonds with maturities of ten years and longer were ahead an average of 5.7 percent annually.

That was not as good as the stock market, and $1,000 invested back then would only have grown to $3,027. But in the shorter term, bonds did better with an average annual five-year gain of 3.8 percent.

This tells you a lot about basic investing. If you want to earn the most money, stocks are the better choice over the long term, but they are more risky. Bonds are safer, but you won't earn as much over time.

By the way, the best place for money over the past twenty years was stocks in developing countries—China, India, Brazil, and the like. They gained an average of 7.8 percent a year. A $1,000 investment would have been worth $4,520 at the end of 2011.

Q: What is the highest number of bill in the world?—*Sydney, age thirteen*

A: It is believed to be the $100 trillion bill issued by the African country of Zimbabwe in January 2009. That may seem like a lot of money, but it would only buy about the same amount as $4 Canadian because of the terrible hyperinflation Zimbabwe experienced.

Q: How do I save money for university? —*Michael, age fifteen*

A: Step one is to get a job. If you don't earn any money, you can't save any. Once you have a job, step two is to decide how much you are going to save from your earnings and then make sure you do it. If you haven't saved a lot already, you should plan to put at least half your salary in the bank. Step three is to see if you can get some help. Your parents probably support your plan to go to college and would undoubtedly be happy to see you pay some of the costs yourself. Ask them if they are willing to match your savings dollar for dollar. If they agree, it would be an incentive for you to save even more.

Q: What are derivatives?
—Jack, age fifteen

A: We certainly didn't expect to run into a question like this from the kids but there it was. Many parents probably don't know the answer so here it is.

A derivative is an artificial security that has no intrinsic value. It only exists because of an underlying security, such as a stock, bond, commodity, or currency. Some people call them "parasites," and the comparison is apt.

To give an example, an option is a type of derivative. It gives you the right to buy or sell a security, let's say a stock, within a specific time for a specific price. You pay a premium to buy the option and if you don't use it by the end date, it expires worthless.

Suppose you decided to buy a call option to purchase 100 shares of High Excitement Gaming Company at $5 a share by May 15. You pay $25 for the option. If High Excitement shares go over $5 before May 15, let's say to $6, you exercise the option and make a $75 profit ($1 on each of 100 shares minus the $25 premium you paid). If High

Excitement never hits $5 before the option expires you lose your $25.

Besides options, the most common types of derivatives are futures, warrants, forward contracts, and swaps.

8
WHAT NEXT? FINANCIAL COURSES AND CAMPS

* *

Students who both took comprehensive financial literacy courses and had good experiences with them perform better when it comes to positive financial attitudes, behaviour, and knowledge.

—THE NATIONAL REPORT CARD
ON YOUTH FINANCIAL LITERACY

In order to be successful, young entrepreneurs need a foundation of knowledge about money management, the role of business in our society, and the important role technology plays.

—STEPHEN ASHWORTH, PRESIDENT AND CEO (ACTING)
OF JUNIOR ACHIEVEMENT CANADA

So once you've finished reading this book, where do you go next with your child's financial education? Well, if you live in Ontario, Manitoba, British Columbia, or Prince Edward Island, your kid will have a leg up on the rest of the country. These provincial governments have all committed to adding financial literacy to the school curriculum. In addition, there's a wide range of financial courses available to Canadian kids nowadays—and hey, a few of them are even free! Remember, your child's financial education begins at home. Setting a good example, talking to your children about household spending, teaching them how to avoid credit and how to spend and save responsibly is ultimately up to you. Kids need a solid foundation on which to build their financial houses. Parents can't sit back and expect schools or camps to do the job for them.

Here are a few suggestions to get you started. Costs are as of summer 2012.

CAMP MILLIONAIRE

Camp Millionaire is a one-week summer camp program for kids ages eleven to fifteen that "teaches about making, managing and multiplying money." The camp is run by BMO private wealth consultant Jorge Ramos, CFP CLU— a man with a passion for finance, an infectious enthusiasm for teaching, and a natural way with kids.

> Location: Toronto, Ontario
> Age level: Grades 6-10
> Cost: $240–$280/week
> Website: www.financialiq.ca

Graduates of Camp Millionaire who are clamouring for more can sign up for the next level of financial literacy camp called Wealth Rules (Grades 9–12).

. . . .

Visiting Camp Millionaire

We dropped in on the innovative Camp Millionaire, held on the Seneca College campus in Toronto, in the summer of 2011. It was a small group of kids, but they were bright, sharp, competitive, and eager as colts. The walls of the classroom were covered with sound-bite style money slogans such as

"You are the CEO of your own life."

"Money is a tool to reach your dreams."

"Assets feed you; liabilities eat you."

Don't be fooled into thinking your kids are in for a dry week of numbers and ratios. On the day of our visit, they were putting on their own version of CBC's *Dragons' Den*. The campers were divided into five groups of four members. Each group was given the task of coming up with an idea for a new business and drafting a business plan along with a sales pitch to be presented to a panel of their peers. Each business proposal was graded on the following criteria:

1. Clarity of business idea
2. Uniqueness of business idea
3. What problem does your business solve?
4. Why are you the best person to run this business?
5. How do you make money?
6. Who's your client?
7. Who are your competitors?
8. Presentation skills
9. Quality of visual aids

On the day of our visit, the winning business plan had the idea of combining a daycare with a professional baby photography service. "Busy moms, come get your child's portraits taken while she's in our care." Brilliant stuff! Along with learning about how to set up a business, the camp teaches about investing, saving, budgeting, credit scores, real estate, the stock market, and money management. Although this camp isn't free, for kids who don't mind spending a week of their summer indoors, it's a great way to jump-start their financial education in a fun, energy-filled environment.

· ·

BIZ TEENS SUMMER CAMP

Your teen can learn entrepreneurial skills such as marketing, team building, budgeting, and making a business plan within the fun atmosphere of a camp setting. Included in the itinerary are field trips and an end-of-camp bazaar where kids can "market" their products.

Location: Vaughan, Ontario
Age level: 12–14
Cost: $150/week
Website: www.recenrollvaughan.ca

GIRLS INC. ECONOMIC LITERACY

This program introduces girls to basic economic and financial concepts, including money management, investments, and global economics.

Location: Girls Inc. organizations are located in
Ontario and Alberta

Age level: 6–18

Cost: Contact your local Girls Inc. for more
information on the availability of this program in
your area.

Website: www.girlsinc.org

MONEY SMARTS 4 KIDS DAY CAMP

Money Smarts 4 Kids is a financial literacy program that teaches children smart money habits through fun-filled games and activities. Concepts such as pay yourself first; save early, save often; put your money to work for you; spend less than you make; only borrow when it's going to make you money; as well as issues such as ethical choices and giving back to the community are all covered in this program.

Location: Oakville, Ontario

Age level: Regular 9–14; Advanced 10–15

Cost: $329/week

Website: www.moneysmarts4kids.com

CENT$IBLE STUDENTS

Co-founders Jenni Bolton and Caroline Munshaw offer financial literacy workshops for Ontario elementary school students (kindergarten through grade 8) with this program endorsed by the Toronto District School Board Financial Literacy Steering Committee. Cent$ible

Students also offers family workshops for parents who want to learn more on how to tackle money matters on the home front.

> Location: Southern Ontario
> Age level: Kindergarten—Grade 8
> Cost: $225 for a two-hour school workshop
> Website: www.centsiblestudents.ca

FUNNY MONEY

For the past seven years, stand-up comedian James Cunningham has been travelling across the country to teach high-school students about managing their money. Cunningham's hilarity keeps teens engaged as he discusses debt, saving, and investing, as well as offering these young adults a much-needed reality check on their financial future. Cunningham's three money tips for teens could easily be mistaken for the lyrics to a Jay-Z song: "Know Your Flow, Control What You Owe, Invest Some Dough." With the combined sponsorship of the Investor Education Fund, the Cambridge Chamber of Commerce, and the Investment Industry Regulatory Organization of Canada, this 45-minute assembly presentation is offered on a complimentary basis to Canadian high schools.

> Location: Across Canada
> Age Level: Grades 11–12
> Cost: Free
> Website: www.funnymoneyhighschools.com

YOUR MONEY

This free in-class seminar is delivered by volunteer bankers in communities across Canada. Developed by the Canadian Bankers Association in partnership with the Financial Consumer Agency of Canada, the seminar introduces key financial concepts such as budgeting, saving, and credit.

> Location: Across Canada
> Age Level: Grades 10–12
> Cost: Free
> Website: www.yourmoney.cba.ca

FINANCIAL LITERACY FOR YOUTH (FLY) PROGRAM

Founded in 2007, FLY's mission is "to promote financial literacy in high schools by stimulating students' interest in financial literacy and encouraging personal financial responsibility." How do they do this? By offering a comprehensive (and free) financial curriculum created for students by students. The curriculum covers the following topics: Time Value of Money; Debt and Credit; Budgeting; Post-Secondary Transition; Types of Investments; and How to Start Now!

To download the free teacher package, volunteer to become a Teacher Advisor, or start up a mini-FLY club in your high school, visit their website.

FLY also operates an annual conference offering students the opportunity to attend workshops, meet business professionals, and get a clearer picture of what personal finance really means.

Location: Vancouver, BC
Age Level: High School
Cost: FLY's school curriculum is operated on a volunteer basis.
FLY's annual conference is available at a cost of $8–$15 per person.
Website: www.financeforyouth.ca

DOLLARS WITH SENSE

This volunteer program run by Junior Achievement Canada offers junior high school students personal money management skills by encouraging them to make sense of their dollars and cents.

From the origins of trade to the ins and outs of investing, Dollars with Sense provides young people with the experience they need to make better economic decisions. Students play an investment strategies game to learn about effective spending and how to avoid credit and debt pitfalls. This interactive program is run by trained volunteer business professionals.

Location: Across Canada
Age Level: Grades 7–9
Cost: Free
Website: www.jacan.org

JUNIOR ACHIEVEMENT COMPANY PROGRAM

This student venture inspires high school students to understand the role of business in our society by having them create an enterprise of their own. By collaborating with professional volunteer consultants to design, organize, and operate a real business, students experience how a small enterprise functions. These new entrepreneurs work within the structure of our Canadian economic system and realize the benefits it provides.

Location: Across Canada
Age Level: Grades 9–12
Cost: Free
Website: www.jacan.org

MONEY SCHOOL CANADA

Money School Canada offers a three-hour Financial Basics workshop program, which is taught by financial services professionals in easily digestible, highly memorable, one-hour weekly sessions. Tailored specifically to students in elementary grades through to high school, this comprehensive in-class program covers the essentials of money management including Financial Goal Setting & Saving; What Banks Do; How Banks Make Money; Interest; Budgeting; Borrowing and Credit. The Financial Basics workshop program receives top marks from students and teachers, delivers an outstanding 25% average improvement in student money management knowledge (in just three in-class hours) and is endorsed by the TDSB Financial Literacy Steering Committee.

Location: Greater Toronto Area (with plans to
expand nationally)
Age Level: Grades 4–11
Cost: $600 for three hours of in-class workshops
Website: www.moneyschoolcanada.com

9
PUTTING IT ALL TOGETHER

· ·

Whether we like it or not, we are our children's
main source of financial information so it is
important for us to be role models.
—CAROLINE MUNSHAW, CENT$IBLE STUDENTS

Now it's in your hands. All the tools you should need
to give your children a financial head start in life
are in this book. You have the knowledge, you have the
techniques, and you have many ways to make the whole
learning experience fun for everyone. Now all you need is
the will power, the discipline, and the cooperation of your
kids to do it.

We won't sugar coat this. It won't always be easy. Your
kids won't always react or behave in the way you hope.
Some may be reluctant to sit still for your "lessons" no
matter how hard you try to make them interesting. Some
may adopt an approach that can only be described as "just
give me the money and shut up." At times, you and your
significant other may disagree on what to do.

But let's face it—that's all part of the joys and frustra-
tions of child-raising. It comes with the territory. No one

ever suggested that rearing a child is easy. It's one of the greatest challenges we will face in our lifetimes. But we do it because we love the kids, and we want them to grow up to be good, successful, and independent. Helping them understand the intricacies of money is an essential part of the process.

So to close this book, let's quickly review the most important points you need to impart to your children at each age level.

AGES FIVE TO SIX

These are the formative years and the time when your children will be most receptive to your guidance. They are curious and eager to learn so take advantage of the opportunity. Here are the key skills they need to have mastered before they reach their seventh birthday:

Counting
The value of coins and how to recognize them
How to shop
Basic budgeting

The biggest skill *you* need to master is how to answer their many questions. That's a real art.

AGES SEVEN TO EIGHT

By now, your child's interest in money has been truly awakened. He's interested in learning more and in having more money of his own to spend. He'll want more practical, real-life experience. Here is what he needs to know at this stage:

> The value of bills
> How to make change
> The effect of sales tax
> Wants versus needs
> How to handle an allowance
> Banking basics
> Saving and sharing

That may seem like a lot, but this is a critical age in your child's financial development. If he gets these skills right at this time, they'll stay with him for the rest of his life.

AGES NINE TO ELEVEN

Now that the kids have hit the tween years, they're starting to think big. Their appreciation of the value of money and the things it can buy has moved to a new level. It's no longer about comic books and Slushies; now they want cellphones and iPods. Those things cost a lot, so it's time the kids learned where to get the money and how to handle it. Here is what they need to know:

The difference between "good" and "bad" spending

How to distinguish between information and
   advertising

How to manage a bank account

The purpose and use of a debit card

How ATMs work

Preparing and following a personal budget

If you've been handling things well, by the time your child reaches her twelfth birthday she will be a sophisticated shopper with her own bank account and debit card.

AGES TWELVE TO THIRTEEN

Until now, most of your child's money has probably come from Mom and Dad. Now they're at the point where it's time to start thinking about earning some for themselves. With that will come more independence and greater responsibility. They will need these skills to be able to cope:

The self-discipline to pay some of their own bills

The ability to find money-earning opportunities
   outside the home

A knowledge of investment basics

An understanding of the difference between money
   and happiness

This may be your last opportunity to ensure your kids have a well-developed sense of financial responsibility. If you have not been able to instil it in them before they hit their mid-teens, it could be too late.

AGES FOURTEEN TO SEVENTEEN

If all has gone well, your child has a good understanding of the financial world at this point. Now it's a matter of refining it and honing the skills you have worked so hard to develop over the years. Here are the final lessons that need to be taught:

Understanding debt and the damage "bad" debt can cause
How to get that first "real" job
Tax and its impact on a paycheque
The value of an RRSP and how to invest the money
Saving for university
Starting a business

At the end of it all, hopefully your child is money-savvy, responsible, and motivated to succeed. If you've really done your job well, you may even have a future millionaire in your family—perhaps the next Bill Gates or Oprah Winfrey. But even if that doesn't happen, you'll have the satisfaction of knowing you did the best you could and that you've given your child every chance for a secure and financially independent future. Combine that with strong moral standards, family love, and a good education, and she couldn't expect anything more.

These are the things we wish for our own children and grandchildren. We hope that you, and we, can achieve them.

INDEX

· · · · · · ·